Interesting but

The Pueblo Revolt of 1680

poorly written

THE PUEBLO REVOLT
OF 1680

Conquest and Resistance in
Seventeenth-Century New Mexico

Andrew L. Knaut

University of Oklahoma Press : Norman

Library of Congress Cataloging-in-Publication Data

Knaut, Andrew L., 1964–
    The Pueblo Revolt of 1680 : conquest and resistance in seventeenth-
century New Mexico / Andrew L. Knaut.
        p.   cm.
    Includes bibliographical references and index.
    ISBN 0-8061-2727-9 (alk. paper, hardcover)
    ISBN 0-8061-2992-1 (alk. paper, paperback)
    1. Pueblo Revolt, 1680. 2. Pueblo Indians—History—17th cen-
tury—Sources. 3. Pueblo Indians—Government relations. 4. New
Mexico—History—17th century—Sources. I. Title.
E99.P9K59   1995   94-23666
                                                                 CIP

Text design by Cathy Carney Imboden. Text typeface is Janson Text 55.

The paper in this book meets the guidelines for permanence and
durability of the Committee on Production Guidelines for Book Lon-
gevity of the Council on Library Resources, Inc. ∞

3   4   5   6   7   8   9   10

To my parents,
Donald and Louise Knaut

Contents

Contents

Illustrations

Preface

This book is, above all else, an attempt to tell a story. Since the early decades of the twentieth century, historians of the Spanish Borderlands have struggled to reconstruct New Mexico's seventeenth-century experience in a way that displays with due prominence the actions and motivations of its most numerous and yet historically almost silent participants, the Pueblo Indians. Any scholar who has faced the task can attest to its difficulty. Because they were nonliterate in pre-modern times, the people of the five major language groups — Piro, Hopi, Zuñi, Tano (including its three subgroups, Tiwa, Tewa, and Towa), and Keresan — known collectively as the Pueblo Indians of northern New Mexico have left little tangible record of their early past. For this reason, historians, ethnohistorians, and anthropologists alike have relied on two major sources of information in their

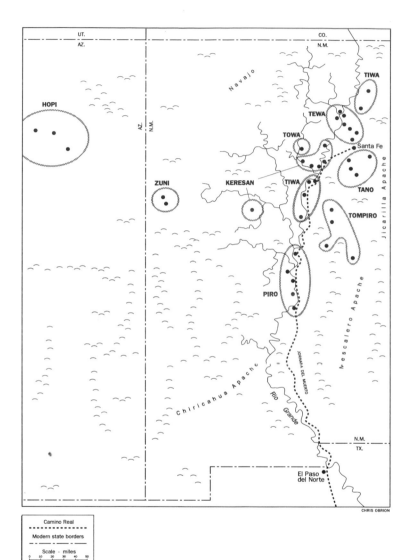

Map 1. Major language groups in seventeenth-century New Mexico

efforts to reconstruct the Pueblo world of the early historical period: interpretations of Pueblo tradition by way of
ethnographic studies begun in the late nineteenth and early
twentieth centuries, and — with careful scrutiny — the documentary record left by Spanish missionaries, settlers, and
colonial officials who lived among the Indians.

Both approaches to the Pueblo past are fraught with
difficulties. Modern-day ethnographers are forced to con-
tend with the fact that centuries of intervening history have
clouded the collective Pueblo memory of the early years of
contact with European intruders, distorting to an indeter-
minable degree the folk tales and ceremonial practices
handed down from generation to generation. At the same
time, the documentary record for early colonial New Mexico reflects all too faithfully the biases of Spanish observers
rarely concerned with conveying an accurate sense of the
lives of their Pueblo vassals. Compounding the problems of
relying on this type of evidence, many of the documents
generated in New Mexico during the seventeenth century
burned in the revolt itself, as Pueblos eager to erase all
vestiges of the Spanish presence in their land torched
mission chapter houses across the province and the government archive in Santa Fe.

The question remains, then, how can one make the
Pueblo experience speak? The issue is addressed in a recent
essay by noted Borderlands historian Elizabeth A. H. John.
Herbert Bolton, writes John, was the first to recognize in
the early twentieth century the need to unearth and recount the Native American story in what is today the
southwestern United States. Trapped by the historio-
graphical constraints of his time, this patriarch in the study
of New Spain's northern fringe rarely managed to venture
beyond his research into the nature of Spanish institutions

and seek a way in which to flesh out the land's historical picture with tales of the Amerindian experience. As a result, "he was unable to realize his dream of 'Parkmanizing' the Borderlands — that is, to win its rightful place in the national epic by writing sagas as attractive to general readers as the Parkman classics."[1] Decades later, the issue of capturing the Indian role in shaping events in the region and of weaving that story into the written history of the Borderlands continues to confront historians, even though a few scholars have taken important steps towards that goal.[2]

This book is an attempt to advance this process one step further. As the climactic event of almost a century and a half of Pueblo-Spanish interaction in the northern Rio Grande basin, the Pueblo Revolt of 1680 is the logical focal point for any examination of seventeenth-century New Mexico. And in spite of the tragic loss of so much documentation from the period, a substantial collection of information survives today in accessible form, thanks largely to the work of a number of Borderlands historians in the first half of the twentieth century. Bolton himself spearheaded the effort to cull surviving documents pertinent to the region's history from archives in Mexico and Spain and present them in an organized form, often translated and published, for use by subsequent generations of scholars.[3] Historians such as Charles W. Hackett, George P. Hammond, Agapito Rey, and France V. Scholes carried on this task in subsequent decades, recovering much of New Mexico's seventeenth-century documentary past and building the invaluable body of material upon which their own and much of the later scholarship in the field has rested.

These resources form the backbone of the present attempt to glean the Pueblo role in shaping the history of seventeenth-century New Mexico and in carrying out successfully the revolt of 1680. When read closely, the colonial documents provide a rich—if not always intentionally recorded—insight into the lives of the land's native inhabitants under the colonial yoke and lay bare the dynamics that pushed a majority of the Pueblo populace to the pitched fervor of rebellion that broke over the region in August 1680. Based upon this treatment of the documentary sources, the chapters that follow will approach the uprising in two ways.

First, they attempt to carve out a more encompassing perspective on the causative factors of the revolt. Broadly speaking, two general interpretations of the rebellion permeate the existing New Mexican historiography. The thesis most commonly adhered to argues that flexibility and/or a mutually beneficial relationship underscored Pueblo-Spanish relations for much of the seventeenth century, undermining any drive on the part of the Pueblos to rid themselves of European rule. Only in the two decades preceding the revolt, when prolonged famine and epidemic diseases combined with the Europeans' inability to check the aggressions of the region's nomadic Athapaskans and the harsh persecutions of native practices by European overlords, did Pueblo consciousness turn to the idea of violent uprising [4] The pages presented here, particularly those of part II, challenge this view of seventeenth-century New Mexican society and argue that meaningful opposition to the Spanish presence in the land permeated Pueblo circles throughout the period.

Other, earlier works on this chapter in New Mexico's history acknowledge more readily the existence of long-term antagonisms between Pueblo and Spanish communities. But by emphasizing the conflict simply as one between two monolithic bodies—Indian versus European—

these interpretations overlook the complexities of the dynamic at work in the decades leading up to the revolt.[5] In reality, the lines that separated Pueblo Indian from European newcomer in the early part of the century blurred considerably over the ensuing generations, allowing for a fluidity between the two segments of society that belied any clear-cut divisions on the basis of race alone. Internecine rivalries had divided the language groups and subgroups of the Pueblo world in the centuries before European contact, and they continued to do so long after the first permanent Spanish colony was established in the region in 1598. More important, but more difficult to document, the arrival of the Spaniards precipitated internal factionalism within each pueblo over such issues as whether or not to accept and profess the newcomers' proffered religion and the weighing of the benefits against the risks and lost independence that might accompany any collaboration with colonial officials.

The Hispanic community, meanwhile, experienced its own divisiveness and, ultimately, change. Intense political and commercial rivalries within the colonists' ranks played out over the course of the century, destroying any hopes the Europeans may have had of maintaining cohesiveness in their effort to dominate a large Pueblo majority. At the same time, the colonists' small numerical presence and their effective isolation from Spanish-American society to the south left them vulnerable to forces that over time effected deep ethnic and cultural transformations among the newcomers to the northern province.[6] Pueblo and Spaniard found their lives woven together with increasing intricacy as the seventeenth century progressed, subtly altering the relationship of vassal to colonial overlord in the region. In the process, the Pueblos gained new insights into the best means of ridding themselves of an unwanted European presence. Only the unique confluence of these complex and long-term internal factors with the severe external threats to the Pueblos' existence that surfaced in the late 1660s and 1670s would engender the widespread unity and motivation that inspired the events of August 1680.

The second purpose of this work, as stated at the outset of this preface, is simply to tell the story of the Pueblo Revolt of 1680. As one scholar has argued, narrative is clearly the best means of capturing "the immediacy that a story can possess as it connects so persuasively with the human experience."[7] But in crafting that narrative, it is my hope not only to breathe new historical life into the experiences of its central actors — the Pueblo Indians — but also to bring those experiences to the attention of readers unaware of the revolt and its significance in the historical development of the North American continent. If, in doing so, these pages lend momentum to the effort to broaden the appeal of the Borderlands' past, to spark new interest in its study, and, as Elizabeth John puts it, to "write this deeply rooted regional history into our nation's sense of self,"[8] this effort will have proven more than gratifying.

Acknowledgments

A number of people have helped me bring this work to completion, and I gladly take this opportunity to thank them. Comments and suggestions by Joe S. Sando and J. Manuel Espinosa proved extremely useful in the final preparation of this manuscript. Willow Powers of the Museum of Indian Arts and Culture and Laboratory of Anthropology in Santa Fe very graciously shared the efforts that she and many in northern New Mexico have made toward establishing guidelines for the appropriate and responsible use of historical photographs taken among the Pueblos. Similarly, I would like to thank Gilbert Sánchez, Frank Martínez, and the governor's office of San Ildefonso Pueblo; Eddy Martínez and the tribal government of San Juan Pueblo; Ernest M. Vallo, Sr., Governor Reginal T. Pasqual, and the people of Acoma; Leslie Overstreet and the Dib-

ner Library of the Smithsonian Institution; the National Anthropological Archives of the Smithsonian Institution; and the Museum of New Mexico for their assistance and kind permission to reproduce the photographs on the pages that follow. And I will be forever indebted to Chris OBrion for sharing his time and artistic talent in creating the maps of seventeenth-century New Mexico presented here.

It has also been my great fortune over the years to enjoy the guidance, expertise, and encouragement of several faculty members of the department of history at Duke University. Ronald Witt's critiques and helpful suggestions have contributed to shaping this manuscript, for which I sincerely thank him. The earliest seeds of my desire to learn more about the Pueblo Revolt took root in a seminar directed by Sydney Nathans in 1985–86, and I can only hope that his skills as teacher and historian surface in the passages that follow as often and as faithfully as they do in my memory of that rewarding experience. John Jay Te-Paske lent his support to this project from its inception, and I count myself as one of the many graduate students whose lives and love of history owe so much to his influence as professor and mentor. Finally, I will never be able to express fully the depth of my appreciation to Peter H. Wood. Though of course any errors contained herein are mine, any and all that is worthwhile in these pages stems in large part from his patient and insightful assistance and his contagious enthusiasm for bringing the past experiences of the peoples of North America to light.

I could not call these acknowledgments complete without also thanking my wife, Carolyn, for the many ways in which she, too, has been a part of all that has gone into the writing of this book. It is sharing in the experience that truly makes it worthwhile.

The Pueblo Revolt of 1680

August 1680

"Now God and Santa Maria Were Dead"

In the villa of Santa Fe, New Mexico, capital of this kingdom and these provinces, on the ninth day of August, 1680, don Antonio de Otermín, governor and captain general of this kingdom and the provinces of New Mexico for His Majesty, states: That he has just received three messages, one from the reverend father *visitador*, Fray Juan Bernal, another from the father preacher, Fray Fernando de Velasco, and the third from Captain Marcos de Dehezas, *alcalde mayor* and *capitán á guerra* of the jurisdiction of Los Taos, all of which messages notify his lordship that the Christian Indians of this kingdom are convoked, allied, and confederated for the purpose of rebelling, forsaking obedience to His Majesty, and apostatizing from the holy faith; and that they desire to kill the ecclesiastical ministers and all the Spaniards, women, and children, destroying the whole population of this kingdom. . . .

3

> All the nations of this kingdom were now implicated . . .
> forming a confederation with the heathen Apaches so
> that, on the night of the thirteenth of the current month,
> they might carry out their disobedience, perfidious trea-
> son, and atrocities.[1]

Word of the planned revolt had leaked. Reports coming in
from the countryside only confirmed the rumors that had
reached the governor earlier in the day by way of Indian
leaders from the Tano pueblos of Pecos, San Cristóbal, San
Marcos, and La Ciénega, who were sympathetic to the
Spanish cause. They had learned of the proposed rebellion,
they told Otermín, from two messengers sent by the Tewa
pueblo of Tesuque to incite their Tano neighbors to partake in the uprising.

Otermín reacted immediately, dispatching his *maestre
de campo*, Francisco Gómez Robledo, to Tesuque to arrest
the messengers and bring them to Santa Fe for questioning.
At the same time, the governor sent word to the *alcaldes
mayores* of all districts in the province warning them of the
imminent revolt and advising them to take appropriate
precautions. Gómez soon returned with the two Tewas,
who were charged with inciting rebellion and interrogated
through an interpreter. Both testified that they had been
sent in secrecy to spread word of the revolt to the nearby
pueblos, bearing deerskins knotted twice to signify the
number of days intervening before the uprising was to
begin. The interrogation continued:

> Being asked what reason or motive they had for rebelling
> and losing respect for God and obedience to his majesty,
> they replied that they knew nothing because they were
> youths, and that among the old men many *juntas* had been
> held with the Indians of San Juan, Santa Clara, Nambé,
> Soxuaque [Pojoaque], Emex [Jemez], and other nations.
> They said that the most that had come to their knowledge

4

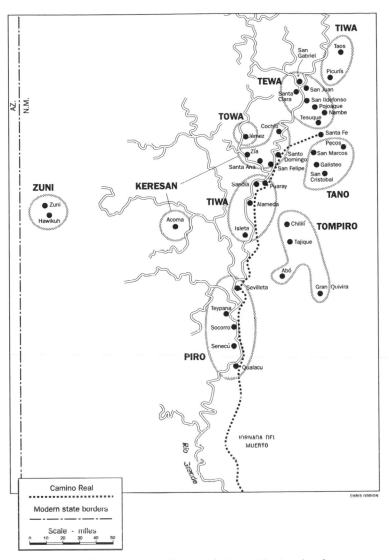

TIWA
San Gabriel
Taos
Picurís
TEWA
Santa Clara
San Juan
San Ildefonso
Pojoaque
Nambe
Tesuque
TOWA
Cochití
Jémez
Zía
Santa Ana
Santo Domingo
San Felipe
Santa Fe
Pecos
San Marcos
Galisteo
San Cristobal
ZUNI
Zuni
Hawikuh
KERESAN
Acoma
Sandía
Puaray
TIWA
Alameda
Isleta
Chililí
Tajique
TANO
TOMPIRO
Abó
Gran Quivira
Sevilleta
Teypana
Socorro
Senecú
Qualacu
PIRO
JORNADA DEL MUERTO
Rio Grande
AZ. N.M.

Camino Real
·······
Modern state borders
Scale - miles
0 10 20 30 40 50

CHRIS ORRION

Map 2. Specific pueblos of central New Mexico in the seventeenth century

is that it is a matter of common report among all the Indians that there had come to them from very far away toward the north a letter from an Indian lieutenant of Pohé-yemu to the effect that all of them in general should rebel, and that any pueblo that would not agree to it they would destroy, killing all the people. . . . They state that they have declared all they know; that it is true that the Indians of San Cristóbal were unwilling to receive the message they brought and reported it to the rest of their nation, which is why it has come to the notice of the señor governor and captain general.[2]

Aware that their plans had been discovered, the Pueblo leaders of the revolt quickly stepped up their timetable for the uprising. At dawn the following day, August 10, a soldier named Pedro Hidalgo left Santa Fe to escort Fray Juan Pío to say mass in the pueblo of Tesuque. Both had heard rumors that one of Tesuque's Hispanic settlers, Cristóbal Herrera, had been killed in the pueblo the night before, so they took caution in their approach. Upon reaching Tesuque, they found the pueblo deserted. Going in search of the missing inhabitants, the two met the Indians in an arroyo a quarter of a league away, making for the surrounding sierras, fully armed and arrayed in war paint.

Pío approached the crowd, crying, "What is this children, are you mad? Do not disturb yourselves; I will die a thousand deaths for you." He then descended into the ravine while Hidalgo rode ahead along a ridge to head off the Tewa exodus. As Hidalgo told the story: "In a little while he saw an Indian named El Obi come out of the ravine with the shield which the said father had been carrying, and he saw also the interpreter of the pueblo, named Nicolás, painted with clay and spattered with blood."[3] Hidalgo himself then fell under attack but managed to escape.

Seeing no further sign of Pío, he assumed the friar dead and rode hard for Santa Fe.

Otermín quickly recognized the danger that now confronted every Hispanic in New Mexico. Isolated in the remote northern colony amid a Pueblo Indian population numbering close to seventeen thousand,[4] the few hundred settlers, soldiers, and Franciscan missionaries in the region faced extinction should the rebellion be allowed to gather momentum. He promptly sent word to all of his alcaldes mayores to raise as many men as possible immediately, ordering them to defend the churches of their respective districts "to prevent their being profaned by the enemy."[5]

Seeking more information, Otermín dispatched a squadron of soldiers to investigate incoming reports of further violence and deaths in the Tewa pueblos of Pojoaque and Cuyamungue. He also sent a messenger to establish contact with his lieutenant governor, Alonso García, in the Río Abajo jurisdiction to the south.[6] The governor then ordered all of the settlers of Santa Fe to gather in the relative safety of the governor's palace and all of the *villa*'s weapons brought out and distributed at once. Arms were to go even to the youths of the settlement, "so that together we can defend ourselves and oppose the enemy if the occasion shall arise."[7] By noon Otermín's orders had been completed. A squad stood guard in the church "for the protection and custody of the holy sacrament and the images, sacred vessels, and things pertaining to divine worship," while sentries and watches took up stations about the *casas reales*.[8]

Over the next two days, reports of uprisings poured in from the northern half of the province. Late in the afternoon of August 10, soldiers Nicolás Lucero and Antonio Gómez reached the governor's palace bearing word from the alcalde mayor of Los Taos that the Indians of Picurís

7

had rebelled. The two had passed through La Cañada on their journey southward, where *sargento mayor* Luis de Quintana told them that at daybreak the natives of Santa Clara Pueblo had attacked a Spanish escort led by Captain Francisco de Anaya, killing two. Quintana had gathered all the Hispanics of the region in his house while a large force of Pueblos of the Tewa and Jemez nations looted the abandoned *estancias* of Santa Clara.[9] On August 12, Francisco Gómez returned from a reconnaissance of the Tewa pueblos and the jurisdiction of La Cañada and reported that

> all the people of the pueblos from Tesuque to San Juan are in rebellion, and a large number of them are fortified in the pueblo of Santa Clara and the rest are in the sierra of the arroyo of Tesuque and scattered along the *camino real*, intercepting the passage of everyone. He says that they have killed Fray Luis de Morales and Fray Tomás de Torres, and that the Indians of Santa Clara have carried off the wife and children of Captain Francisco de Anaya. He found that they have killed, in the pueblo of Pojoaque, Captain Francisco Ximenes, Don Joseph de Goitia, the wife and family of Francisco Ximenes.[10]

And so the list of dead and missing grew. Late in the evening of the August 12, Otermín dispatched a party to aid the Hispanic settlers of Los Cerrillos—besieged in the house of sargento mayor Bernabé Márquez—and escort them to Santa Fe to join those huddled behind the walls of the casas reales.[11]

On August 13, the situation worsened for the settlers of Santa Fe. Throughout the day, reports of deaths and atrocities poured in from the surrounding countryside. Also, Otermín received confirmation that despite the early pro-Spanish leanings of their leaders, many of the natives of La

Ciénega, San Marcos, and Pecos had joined the rest of the region in revolt. Adding to the fear within the villa was news that throughout the province the Pueblos had captured the better part of the settlers' horse herds, the "principal nerve of warfare" in the region.[12] Equally distressing, no word had yet come from the messenger dispatched three days previously to reach Alonso García and the settlers of Río Abajo.

Otermín now prepared for the worst. He sent a final dispatch to Alonso García asking the lieutenant governor for any aid possible in the way of men and horses in the hope that somehow the message would get through. He then summoned Luis de Quintana and his settlers in La Cañada to Santa Fe and instructed them to bring whatever horses and cattle they still possessed. Shortly thereafter, Otermín commanded the entrenchment of the casas reales in preparation to withstand a siege, and, "foreseeing that all the nations [of the province] will join together and destroy this villa," he ordered Fray Francisco Gómez de la Cadena to "consume the most holy sacrament, and take the images, sacred vessels, and things appertaining to divine worship, close the church and convent, and bring everything to the palace."[13]

Further word of the peril facing the Hispanic community and a hint of the underlying cause of the uprising reached Otermín on the morning of the fourteenth, when two Indian messengers dispatched the previous day returned with the news that

> all the Indians of the pueblos of Los Pecos, San Cristóbal, San Lázaro, San Marcos, Galisteo, and La Ciénega, who numbered more than five hundred, were one league from this villa [of Santa Fe] on the way to attack it and destroy the governor and all the Spaniards, so that the whole

9

kingdom might be theirs, and they might profit at the expense of the Spaniards and their haciendas. They were saying that now God and Santa Maria were dead, that they were the ones whom the Spaniards worshiped, and that their own God whom they obeyed had never died.[14]

The two messengers reported that the rebels awaited reinforcements from the natives of Taos, Picurís, and all of the Tewa pueblos, as well as from the Apaches.[15]

Pueblo forces appeared on the plains surrounding Santa Fe on the morning of August 15 and soon occupied the houses on the outskirts of the villa with the intent of besieging the casas reales. During the day one of Otermín's reconnaissance parties persuaded a leader of the movement to come in and parley with the governor, who immediately asked the Indian why the Pueblos had chosen to revolt. The Indian replied that

> there was now no help for it; that everything said about the deaths of the father custodian and all the other Spaniards and religious was true, and that the Indians who were coming with him and those whom they were awaiting were coming to destroy the villa. They were bringing two crosses, one red and the other white, so that his lordship might choose. The red signified war and the white that the Spaniards would abandon the kingdom.[16]

In response, Otermín returned the emissary to his followers with an offer of full pardon for all those involved in the revolt if they returned peacefully to their pueblos and reaffirmed their submission to Christianity and the Spanish crown. The Pueblos responded with jeers and signaled for the battle to begin.[17]

The Indians now moved in, setting fire to the outskirts of the villa and the church of San Miguel. Otermín answered by leading his entire force—fewer than one hundred men[18] — out to counter the advance. The battle that ensued, as Otermín recalled, lasted most of the day, "during which many of the enemy were killed and they wounded many of our men, because they came with the harquebuses and the arms which they had taken from the religious and the Spaniards, and were very well provided with powder and shot."[19] Otermín's forces inflicted numerous casualties upon the Pueblo forces, but the arrival late in the afternoon of reinforcements from Taos, Picurís, and the Tewa pueblos tore victory from the governor's grasp. Darkness fell with Otermín and his troops withdrawing to the palace and the Pueblos gaining a position behind the casas reales from which they could fire into the plaza of the governor's home.[20]

At this point a stand-off ensued that lasted until August 18, when the Pueblos — whose ranks now exceeded twenty-five hundred[21] — cut the water supply to the villa. Desperate from a thirst that had lasted two days and a night, Otermín conferred with his officers late the following day and concluded that "it would be a better and safer step to die fighting than of hunger and thirst, shut up within the casas reales."[22] On the morning of August 20 the governor charged forth from the palace leading all the soldiers he could muster. A rout followed in which the Spaniards dislodged the Pueblos from the villa, killing three hundred, capturing forty-seven, and setting the remaining thousands to flight. Hostilities ended before noon with five Spaniards dead and many wounded, including Otermín, shot once in the face and once in the chest. The governor interrogated the forty-seven prisoners briefly that afternoon before summarily executing them under the charge of treason.[23]

On the following day, Otermín drew up an *auto* stating that

11

it is known that from Los Taos to the pueblo of Isleta, which is a distance of fifty-one leagues, all the people, religious, and Spaniards have perished, no other persons being alive except those who found themselves besieged within the *casas reales* of the villa, and there is information to the effect that the residents of Río Abajo have fortified themselves and assembled in the said pueblo of Isleta. For which reasons, and finding ourselves out of provisions, with very few horses, weary, and threatened by the enemy, and not being assured of water . . . [it is decided] to withdraw, marching from this villa in full military formation until reaching the pueblo of La Isleta, where it is said that the residents of Río Abajo are gathered with the lieutenant general of that jurisdiction.[24]

The decision made, Otermín hurried preparations for the march. He deemed it imperative to leave Santa Fe before the Pueblos recovered from their defeat and attacked anew, and before the persistent rumors of the impending arrival of Apache reinforcements proved true.[25] Because many of the settlers had fled their homes with little in the way of provisions, Otermín ordered his possessions to be distributed among the approximately one thousand "Spanish soldiers . . . their families and servants . . . Mexican natives, and all classes of people" gathered within the palace.[26]

The march southward was a difficult one for Otermín and his followers; hunger and persistent fear plagued the refugees. The retreat carried the outcasts to the pueblo of San Marcos on August 23 and along the banks of the Río Grande to reach Sandía on August 26. Signs of the revolt were everywhere. Abandoned pueblos, desecrated churches and religious images, burned and looted estancias, and the bodies of those who had felt the full force of Pueblo fury stood as grim markers of disaster. And always, there were

12

the Indians. Whether from the mesa tops, the far side of the river, or atop horses on the distant plains, the Pueblo presence haunted the unwelcome settlers. At times that presence lashed out to test the fleeing column, feigning attack and provoking more than a few minor skirmishes. Yet for the most part the Pueblos watched, simply noting the progress of the exodus and sending up an occasional smoke signal.[27]

Outside Sandía, Otermín received first word of new disaster. A Pueblo prisoner captured during an altercation near the pueblo informed the governor that

> the lieutenant general of those [Río Abajo] jurisdictions and the religious who had escaped from the district of Sandia as well as from Los Jemez, Zia, and La Isleta, had assembled on the day of the uprising [August 10] in the pueblo of La Isleta, and that from there they had set out with all the residents, none remaining behind, toward El Paso del Río del Norte, intending to go out to El Parral.[28]

At La Isleta on August 27, a vacant pueblo confirmed the prisoner's testimony. García and his followers had left more than two weeks earlier. Otermín's camp was now desperate, without food and barely clothed.[29] The governor had little choice but to press on, sending messengers ahead to order García to halt wherever he might be found.

On September 4, Otermín's scouts overtook García at Fray Cristóbal, a landmark fifty miles south of Socorro. Hitherto unaware that Otermín had survived the revolt, García and six men immediately rode north to meet the governor at El Alamillo on September 6. There Otermín promptly arrested García, charging him with deserting the colony without the governor's permission and ignoring Otermín's orders to send aid to Santa Fe.[30]

13

In his defense, García argued that he had been forced to act on the belief that Otermín and all the settlers of the Río Arriba region had perished in the uprising. None of the governor's messengers had reached García in the opening days of the revolt, and none of the lieutenant governor's own followers had been able to find safe passage across the Pueblo-controlled territory that separated the southern jurisdiction from Santa Fe. García and those around him had therefore agreed that the logical course of action was to take his settlers and proceed south in good military order until they met the caravan of supplies from Mexico City known to be en route up the Río Grande and led by Fray Francisco de Ayeta. Only then, García reasoned, could a properly supplied expedition be mounted to ascertain the fate of the governor and the settlers of the northern half of the province.[31] Satisfied with this defense, Otermín acquitted García of the charges, and the two camps met at Fray Cristóbal on September 13.[32]

On September 19, the band of refugees reached La Salineta, just north of El Paso del Norte. They numbered 1,946 and included 155 Hispanic men and youths considered capable of bearing arms, along with Hispanic women and children. Non-Europeans made up the majority of the group: Indian servants and many of the inhabitants of the Piro pueblos in the southern reaches of the province who, for reasons unknown, had been excluded from the general rebellion by the leaders of the revolt.[33] Otermín estimated the number of settlers dead as a result of the uprising to be 380, of whom 73 were adult males.[34] Also, twenty-one of the province's forty Franciscan friars lay dead at the hands of their Pueblo parishioners.[35]

For the surviving refugees, defeat was complete. Eighty years of a Spanish presence in New Mexico had ended in

14

ruins. The Pueblos, for their part, had accomplished what no other Amerindian society had achieved on such a scale before them, and what none would achieve after — a complete setback of European expansion in the New World.

Part I

Early Contacts in New Mexico

Conquest and Visions of Distance

Intimidation was the key to Spanish authority among the Pueblo Indians of northern New Mexico in the seventeenth century. It was a key that, prior to 1680, was used effectively by what never amounted to more than a handful of Hispanics to lock a Pueblo Indian population numbering in the tens of thousands into a harshly and inconsistently administered Spanish colonial structure.

The earliest seeds of this intimidation took root as a consequence of repeated incursions by Spanish adventurers into the Pueblo world over the course of the sixteenth century. Beginning in 1539, Franciscan missionaries, aspiring conquistadores, and profit-hungry entrepreneurs alike found themselves lured into the region from their homes in central Mexico and, later, Nueva Vizcaya by fantastic tales of a large population of town-dwelling Indians to the north. Rumors surfaced periodically to tell of cities beyond the northern frontier that rivaled in size and splendor the recently conquered Aztec capital of Tenochtitlán and the centers of Inca wealth in the central Andes. As dreams of riches and fame pushed the first Spanish expeditions into the region, the native inhabitants watched and suffered as a pattern of violence emerged that would dictate the nature of Pueblo-European interaction throughout the century.

Each new intrusion touched off a cycle in which the Spaniards, unable or unwilling to carry enough provisions to sustain their numbers for extended periods, pressed their Indian hosts for food and clothing and thereby fostered deep resentment toward the newcomers in the Pueblo consciousness.[1] Consistently, that resentment flared into open displays of resistance to Spanish demands, which in turn prompted the Europeans to force native compliance through brutal acts of suppression, poisoning relations even further. Only the intruders' departure broke the cycle, leaving the land's native peoples to tend their wounds and wonder whether and when a new group of unwanted visitors from the south would arrive again.

The sixteenth century drew to a close with the arrival in New Mexico of don Juan de Oñate and his followers, who successfully exploited past Pueblo experiences with Spanish invaders to establish the first permanent European colony in the region in 1598. Oñate hoped to build a lasting respect for colonial authority among the Pueblos and an acceptance of Franciscan friars in their communities. Uprisings by the inhabitants of Acoma in December 1598 and January 1599 and Oñate's carefully calculated response provide important insight into the governor's conception of the best manner in which to achieve his goals. Sharply delineated roles for Spanish settlers and Catholic missionaries aimed at highlighting the punitive capabilities of the former and the benevolence of the latter underscored

18

Oñate's dialectic for dominating the region's overwhelmingly large native population and marked the Spaniards' first tentative steps toward establishing a lasting authority in northern New Mexico.

In the opening years of the seventeenth century, however, internal dissension within the European community would open deep cracks in Oñate's carefully laid foundation and undermine Spanish efforts to build a stable colonial presence in the land for decades to come.

Chapter One

Oñate's *Entrada*

Don Philip . . . to don Juan de Oñate, resident of the city of Zacatecas: In consideration and appreciation of your personal quality and merits and of the services that you rendered for twenty years in the war against the Chichimecan Indians of the Kingdoms of Nueva Galicia and Nueva Vizcaya . . . I appoint you as my governor, captain general, caudillo, discoverer, and pacifier of the . . . provinces of New Mexico and those adjacent and neighboring, in order that, in my royal name, you may enter them with the settlers and armed forces, baggage, equipment, munitions, and other necessary things that you may provide for this purpose. You will endeavor to attract the natives with peace, friendship, and good treatment, which I particularly charge you, and to induce them to hear and accept the holy gospel; you will explain our holy Catholic faith to them through interpreters, if they can

be obtained, so that we may have communication with them in the various languages and seek their conversion; Let it be done at the opportunity which the friars find most suitable. You will see to it that the latter are respected and revered, as ministers of the gospel should be, so that, with this example, the Indians may attend and honor them and accept their persuasions and teachings. Experience has demonstrated this to be very important, and also that all the people in your company act gently and kindly, without committing excesses or setting bad examples, or irritating those we seek to attract lest they adopt an unfriendly attitude toward the faith. You are to direct everything to this principal aim.[1]

With these words, King Philip II of Spain officially sanctioned the opening of the province of New Mexico to colonial expansion in 1595. New Mexico, however, was by no means virgin ground for Spaniards in the final decade of the sixteenth century. Interest in the northern region among would-be conquistadores, profiteers, and Catholic missionaries in central Mexico dated from as early as 1536, when four survivors of Narváez's disastrous 1528 attempt to colonize Florida arrived in Mexico City with tales of their epic six-year trek across much of what is now Texas and the American Southwest.

The most vocal of the travelers, Alvar Núñez Cabeza de Vaca, fired the imaginations of his listeners as he spoke of crossing the river that would come to be known as the Río Grande and there hearing stories of an advanced Indian civilization settled in large and prosperous cities to the north. As corroborative evidence, Cabeza de Vaca presented five malachite arrowheads given to him by a band of Ures Indians during his stay in the region. The stones' green color quickly transformed them into emeralds in the minds of Spaniards eager to believe that a "new" Mexico, a land of untapped wealth rivaling that of recently conquered Tenochtitlán, lay somewhere beyond the northern frontier.[2]

The rumors precipitated a flurry of activity in the viceregal capital. Hernán Cortés set out immediately by sea up the Pacific Coast in a futile attempt to locate the northern riches. The newly arrived viceroy of Nueva España, Antonio de Mendoza, took steps of his own to verify Cabeza de Vaca's reports. Mendoza appointed Fray Marcos de Niza, a Franciscan veteran of the conquest of Peru, as head of a small scouting expedition to be guided north by one of Cabeza de Vaca's traveling companions, the black slave Esteban.[3] The Franciscan's expedition departed from Culiacán, the northernmost Spanish outpost in Nueva España, on March 7, 1539.

Fray Marcos himself saw little of the territory that would later be called New Mexico. Instead, he based much of his testimony about the land on word sent back to him by Esteban, who had struck out in advance of the main party with a few Indian auxiliaries shortly after leaving Culiacán. Esteban's reports painted a glowing and, as it was eventually discovered, greatly exaggerated picture of the wealth and prosperity of the peoples he encountered as he moved north. His inflated accounts eventually spurred the friar to catch up with the advance party in all haste. News of Esteban's death at the hands of the Zuñi inhabitants of Hawikuh, however, forced de Niza to end the expedition and return south. The Franciscan himself caught only a glimpse of the pueblo from a distance before giving the word to retreat, but the image was sufficient for de Niza to conjure up tales of a wondrous site, "larger than the city of Mexico,"[4] upon his return to the capital in September 1539.

Encouraged by the friar's account, Mendoza authorized Francisco Vázquez de Coronado, governor of Nueva Galicia, to lead an expedition of conquest into the northern territory. Coronado's forces—close to three hundred European soldiers and more than eight hundred Mexican Indian auxiliaries pushing herds of a thousand horses and five hundred head of livestock—were large enough to cause concern over the security of the Spaniards left behind after its departure from Mexico City. The expedition headed north from central Mexico in February 1540. Advance forces entered Hawikuh on July 7, 1540, and over the course of the next twenty-three months Coronado and his followers moved extensively throughout the Pueblo world, wintering twice among the Tiwa pueblos in the central Río Grande valley.

As the months passed, the Spaniards found no indications of material wealth in the land or among its peoples, and disillusionment and hardship gradually replaced the expectations of wealth and fame that had fueled the expedition. After two long and difficult winters and a futile journey across the Great Plains in search of gold-laden settlements always rumored to lie just beyond the horizon, Coronado opted to abandon the region and return south in April 1542. For a time, bitter disappointment quieted the powerful European desire to press into the northern province.

Decades passed, though, and as dust slowly covered Coronado's reports in the archives of Mexico City and the royal courts of Spain, gilded mirages reappeared along the northern frontiers of the empire. By the 1580s, the Spanish realm had extended as far as the rich mining country of what is today southern Chihuahua, where frontier towns like El Parral, Santa Bárbara, and Zacatecas attracted profit-seeking entrepreneurs, fugitives from royal justice, and Franciscan friars zealous to push outward in their missionary efforts among the region's Indian groups.

Eventually, the old rumors resurfaced in the area telling of advanced and populous cities to the north, ripe with goods and labor to be exploited and countless souls to be won over to the Christian faith. As a result, the push for a new expedition, or *entrada*, into the region soon began anew.

Since Coronado's time, however, the Spanish crown had changed its attitude toward the exploration and settlement of new territories considerably. Charles V, moved by the pleas of writers like Bartolomé de las Casas and their pointed condemnations of the destruction of the New World's Indian peoples and the abuses of the Spanish colonial system, had in 1542 passed the New Laws aimed at curbing the excesses that had characterized the conquests of the Aztec and Inca realms. On July 13, 1573, Philip II had strengthened that legislation with the Laws of Discovery, which expressly forbade "conquests" in the forms seen in the early days of the American empire and even prohibited the mentioning of the term in conjunction with the colonization of new lands.[5] Spanish subjugation of Indians and their lands was now to be carried out in a Christian and humane manner; the blood baths of the past were to be avoided. Any new foray into the northern territories would henceforth receive royal sanction only under the pretext of establishing missions among the Indians and working to convert them to Catholicism. As the religious order with the strongest presence along the northern frontier, the Franciscans stood to benefit most from this shift in emphasis. They would now play a central role in any attempted settlement of New Mexico.[6]

Under these changed political circumstances, an unusual and symbiotic relationship flourished between Franciscans and a number of well-placed profiteers in the frontier mining towns in the years from 1580 until the close of the century. Keen to press forward into new mission fields, the friars nevertheless recognized that any successful entry into New Mexico depended upon military protection and financial backing that only the region's wealthy entrepreneurs could provide. The latter, sensitive to varying degrees to the crown's changed position with respect to missions of conquest and to the royal edicts forbidding unauthorized expansion beyond the northern borders of the realm, realized that any commercial venture on their part into the new territories would have to be cloaked in the guise of an expedition dedicated to assisting the Franciscans in their efforts to pull more souls into the Christian fold.[7]

The first in the new round of entradas into New Mexico departed Santa Bárbara on June 5, 1581, under the joint leadership of Fray Agustín Rodríguez and Captain Francisco Sánchez Chamuscado.[8] This expedition of nine soldiers, three Franciscan friars, and nineteen Mexican Indian auxiliaries, with six hundred head of livestock and ninety horses, reached the southernmost Piro pueblo in August 1581, only to find the town abandoned by its people out of fear of the approaching Europeans. The group pressed on, eventually making contact with the land's native inhabitants, and over the next several months traveled extensively throughout the Río Grande valley. The party ventured as far as the Keresan pueblos in the north and the Zuñi pueblos and Acoma to the west, and it passed through the Tompiro pueblos east of the Manzano range on its return to Santa Bárbara in the spring of 1582.

The safe return of the expedition on April 15, 1582, sparked excitement and an immediate call to further action in the small mining town. Franciscan officials listened with alarm to the news that two of the friars, Rodríguez and

Francisco López, had elected to remain without military escort in the pueblo of Puaray to begin missionary work among its inhabitants. Concerned for the safety of their brethren, the Franciscans immediately cast about in search of someone willing to lead a mission of rescue into the newly rediscovered territories. Fortune seemed to smile on the friars when they learned that Antonio de Espejo, a wealthy cattle rancher from Querétaro, was in the area and willing to lead such an expedition at his own cost.

Perhaps unbeknownst to the Franciscans, Espejo had fled to Santa Bárbara to escape criminal charges pending against him in Mexico City. The friars' predicament seemed to him to offer the perfect opportunity to go one step further in evading royal justice. At the same time, the entrepreneur could seek out sources of investment and mining prospects in the new land and perhaps even clear his name should he manage to appear as the savior of the two stranded friars. Anxious to get the expedition under way quickly, the Franciscans helped Espejo bypass royal channels in seeking approval to lead the mission by providing him with documentation signed only by a local alcalde mayor. On November 10, 1582, Espejo headed north from Santa Bárbara with fourteen soldiers and one Franciscan friar.[9]

In his travels through New Mexico, Espejo retraced many of the steps taken by Chamuscado and Rodríguez the previous year. Word reached the party early on that the two friars had suffered martyrdom at the hands of Puaray's inhabitants, but Espejo continued his explorations and his search for signs of mineral wealth that would make a future large-scale colonization of the land profitable. After finding some evidence of copper deposits in the mountains west of the Hopi pueblos, Espejo returned south, reaching the frontier on September 10, 1583.[10]

26

There, his soon-exaggerated tales of New Mexico's wealth and its prosperous Indian population sparked two more expeditions into the region, both undertaken without sanction by royal authorities in Mexico City and Madrid. In 1590, Gaspar Castaño de Sosa made headway in establishing an unauthorized Spanish colony among the Pueblos, only to be recalled the following year by royal officials for violating the crown's colonization laws. Similarly, Captain Francisco Leyva de Bonilla attempted an illegal entrada into New Mexico in 1593 but eventually lost his life at the hands of his own men during an expedition to the Great Plains. An unidentified group of Plains Indians killed the remaining Europeans of the party shortly afterward.[11]

The Pueblo Indians of northern New Mexico could now claim more than half a century of experience with European intruders. As wave after wave of unwanted visitors had passed through the land, each had managed to leave an indelible impression upon the region's native inhabitants, and not a few scars.

The earliest contact with outsiders—Esteban's 1539 visit to Hawikuh—had revealed the newcomers' true intent and charted a course for Pueblo-Spanish relations that was followed again and again with each subsequent arrival of the Europeans and their followers. The Zuñi inhabitants of Hawikuh had watched in amazement as the dark-skinned wanderer trampled without hesitation over the corn meal spread across the entryway to the village, a sacred welcome for travelers from the pueblo whose return from a pilgrimage coincided with Esteban's intrusion in May 1539. Not satisfied with the greeting extended to him by the pueblo's leaders, the stranger then demanded gifts of turquoise and women, warning his hosts that many of his brethren would soon follow and "that they had numerous

27

arms."[12] After three days of careful deliberation, the angered Zuñi leaders decided that only by killing this insolent visitor could they rid themselves of his presence and ensure that word of the pueblo's location never reached his followers to the south.[13]

The arrival of Coronado and his large force at Hawikuh the following year, however, soon proved the futility of the Zuñi resistance. Village leaders had hoped to halt the intruders with yet another line of corn meal spread across the entrance to the pueblo. When this proved ineffective, they refused to acquiesce to Spanish demands for food and clothing, an act that prompted Coronado to sack Hawikuh on July 7, 1540.[14] Coronado and his followers would repeat the scenario at Hawikuh often in their travels over the next two years. Unable to carry provisions sufficient to feed and clothe such a large expeditionary force, the Spaniards depended instead upon the Pueblos—particularly the Tiwas of the central Río Grande valley—to house and supply them during the difficult winters of 1540–41 and 1541–42. Pedro de Castañeda, a member of Coronado's forces, highlighted the stress that these demands placed upon the Pueblos when he told of an incident in which Coronado called on the leader of one of the Tiwa pueblos for supplies:

> The General spoke with [the Tiwa leader], asking him to furnish three hundred or more pieces of clothing which he needed to distribute to his men. He replied that it was not in his power to do this . . . that they had to discuss the matter among the pueblos, and that the Spaniards had to ask this individually from each pueblo. . . . As there were twelve [Tiwa] pueblos . . . as soon as a Spaniard came to a pueblo, he demanded the supplies at once, and they had to give them, because he had to go on to the next one. With all this there was nothing the natives could do

except take off their own cloaks and hand them over until the number that the Spaniards asked for was reached. Some of the soldiers who went along with these collectors, when the latter gave them some blankets or skins that they did not consider good enough, if they saw an Indian with a better one, they exchanged it with him without any consideration or respect, and without inquiring about the importance of the person they despoiled. The Indians resented this very much.[15]

That resentment flared into open resistance several times during Coronado's years among the Pueblos, as the region's inhabitants lost patience with these strangers who took what was not offered them and never gave of themselves. The people of Arenal, for example, chose to defy the Spaniards' demands for provisions, a stance that prompted the Europeans to torch the pueblo and burn thirty of its inhabitants at the stake. In all, Coronado attacked and destroyed thirteen of the fifteen or so Tiwa pueblos in the region over the course of the two winters, leaving a first impression of the European intruders that few Pueblos would forget over the ensuing decades.[16]

By the time of the Chamuscado-Rodríguez expedition in 1581, memories of Coronado's brutalities continued to burn in the Pueblo consciousness. As this new group of explorers entered the region, they found the southernmost Piro pueblos abandoned, their inhabitants having fled upon hearing news of the return of the Europeans.[17] The Pueblos' instincts proved well founded, for this and every subsequent foray into the land by well-armed but poorly provisioned adventurers brought with it a new round of Spanish demands and harsh repressions of any show of native resistance. In September 1581, the Tano inhabitants of Malajón killed three of the horses of the Chamuscado-Rodríguez party in frustration over the intruders' continual extortion of food and clothing. The Europeans retaliated by burning the pueblo and killing many of its people.[18] Two years later, members of the Espejo expedition seized and garroted sixteen inhabitants of Puaray and burned a number of the pueblo's kivas, killing the people huddled inside as a stern warning against withholding goods from the white men.[19] Castaño de Sosa took similar steps to punish the people of Pecos for refusing his demands for corn during his travels through New Mexico in 1590.[20]

By the middle of the 1590s, royal officials were well aware of the atrocities committed against the natives of New Mexico by these early Spanish adventurers and—unaware of the deaths of the members of the Leyva de Bonilla party—believed the mistreatment to be continuing daily.[21] The crown, anxious to establish a controlled and lasting presence in the region, recognized that if respect for Spanish prestige and the Catholic faith were ever to be instilled among the Indians, brutalities of the sort committed by these small parties of renegades in their shortsighted efforts to force the Indians' immediate submission had to stop.

Practical concerns alone dictated more humane treatment of New Mexico's inhabitants. Any further damage to the "prestige of our nation among the Indians of that land,"[22] wrote viceroy Luis de Velasco, only undermined the possibility that a handful of colonists and missionaries might one day pacify and live in peace among a Pueblo Indian populace that early estimates had numbered in the hundreds of thousands.[23] The circumstances called for cunning, not brutality, and an understanding that "as the Indians are so much more numerous than the Spaniards, resort must be had to strategy, and so the soldiers must be brave and bold . . . and chosen by the governor immediately in charge of the expedition who is able to visualize its problems."[24] The governor himself needed to be a man "clever, skillful, and industrious," well experienced in Indian affairs, and able to "pay more particular attention to the service of God our Lord and mine and the general welfare of the natives than his own personal interest."[25]

There was no shortage of wealthy entrepreneurs willing to finance and lead the official entrada into New Mexico. Enticed by rumors of the land's richness that grew in proportion almost daily along the northern frontier, many believed the enterprise to be a sure means of building fame and personal fortune. Don Juan de Oñate, a personal acquaintance of viceroy Luis de Velasco and the son of Cristóbal de Oñate, a former governor of Nueva Galicia and one of the founders of Zacatecas, emerged early as a strong contender in the competition. Heir to his father's substantial mining legacy and a veteran of the Chichimeca wars, Oñate soon found favor in royal circles for heading the entrada. On September 21, 1595, Velasco accepted his bid to head an expedition of two hundred men and their dependents at his own expense.[26]

The instructions given to Oñate regarding the conduct and composition of his settlers were strict, tailored to reverse Pueblo preconceptions of the Spaniards as ragtag looters and murderers. Velasco stressed the royal edicts forbidding harsh treatment of the Indians. To prevent theft of food and supplies from the natives during the expedition, he warned Oñate repeatedly to provision his men amply.[27] Pillaging of Pueblo stores and possessions could only accentuate feelings of hostility toward the Spaniards and jeopardize Oñate's mission to establish a permanent Spanish presence in the region. Royal officials clearly understood that "in truth the initial success of the expedition will not depend so much on their number as their discipline and on being so well provisioned that they can support themselves for some time."[28] Colonial authorities also paid close attention to the types of men and women who filled Oñate's ranks, requiring him to register all persons of mestizo blood among the colonists and barring him from bringing "negro slaves, who mistreat the Indians and whom they fear for the harm they cause them."[29] Finally, Velasco ordered Oñate to seek out and arrest the renegade Leyva de Bonilla and his followers, still believed to be at large in New Mexico, in the hope of demonstrating clearly to the natives that such reprehensible conduct was not sanctioned by Spanish authorities.[30]

His contract approved and his orders received in 1595, Oñate quickly assembled his two hundred men and the needed supplies in Santa Bárbara. Administrative delays, however, allowed debate over Oñate's suitability to conduct the expedition to arise in the royal courts and postponed the entrada. For Oñate and his men, weeks of waiting for final approval stretched into months, and months into years. Oñate's supplies, so vital to the success of the expedition, dwindled, and his men slowly drifted from the camp.[31] Finally Oñate received the order to proceed, and on February 7, 1598, the expedition set out, its supplies low and its numbers reduced to 129 of the 200 men promised. Seven Franciscan friars and two lay brothers accompanied the northward-bound convoy. On April 30, 1598, this latest group of adventurers completed the crossing of the Río Grande below what is today El Paso–Juárez, and Oñate took possession of the province of New Mexico in the name of King Philip II of Spain.[32] Spaniards had entered Pueblo lands once again.

Signs of the Pueblos' bitter experiences with past Spanish expeditions greeted Oñate almost from the moment he crossed into the northern province. The inhabitants of the southern Piro pueblos, alerted to the arrival of yet another band of white-skinned intruders, fled to the surrounding hill country as Oñate's advance parties approached. The first tentative contacts between members of the expedition and the land's native peoples revealed what was by now a firmly entrenched legacy among the Pueblos of wariness toward the newcomers and appeasement of their strange ways. In later travels through the Hopi pueblos in the west, Oñate and his men would encounter natives whom

> they called the Crossed Ones, because of crosses that each of them, large and small, wear on their foreheads . . . whenever the Spaniards approach. For the origin of this mystery, it is known how many years ago a religious of the Franciscan Order passed through that land who told them that if at any time they were to see white men with beards, if they did not want them to treat them badly, they should put on those crosses, which are a thing which they [the Spaniards] esteem. They took this to memory and have not forgotten it.[33]

Capitalizing on the reluctance of the Pueblos to contest the expedition's presence in the land, Oñate moved swiftly up the Río Grande valley and halted at the Tewa pueblo of Yunge Oweenge, where the town's inhabitants vacated their homes and offered no resistance as the Spaniards occupied the village and renamed it San Juan de los Caballeros.[34]

As daily contacts between Europeans and Pueblos increased, the Spaniards found themselves astounded by the Indians' unwillingness to challenge the newcomers, and several chose to perceive this as evidence of an unusual civility inherent among New Mexico's aboriginal inhabitants. Fray Francisco de Escobar called the Pueblos "very affable and docile," noting that "they all live in pueblos which, for Indian dwellings, are very well arranged. . . . They are satisfied with little, but they do not have enough."[35] These peaceful people seemed virtually free from vice in the European sense of the word, one colonist noted, since

> their houses are always open and have no doors or other protection, because the practice among them is never to take anything from each other. . . . When one of the soldiers lost a jewel and an Indian found it and learned whose it was, he returned it of his own accord without compulsion. This is the common practice among all of these Indians.[36]

Another wrote that the Pueblos "are so peaceful and obedient that they all answer to his [Oñate's] call and summons when a lone Indian messenger visits them with a small notebook belonging to the governor."[37]

More cognizant of the intimidation that had hitherto underpinned the successes of the expedition, Oñate carefully reinforced the Pueblos' respect for Spanish military might through a number of public "celebrations" that included well-choreographed reenactments of Spanish victories over the Moors and—closer to Pueblo consciousness—at Tenochtitlán in 1519–23.[38] Pressing his advantage further, the governor traveled throughout the province in the summer and fall of 1598, periodically gathering Indian captains whom he judged to represent the surrounding Pueblo groups and, via double translation,[39] receiving uncontested pledges of vassalage and obedience. "By doing so," Oñate wrote, "they would live in peace, justice, and orderliness, protected from their enemies, and benefitted in the arts and trades and in their crops and cattle."[40] By

October 1598, he had moved throughout the western pueblos as well, accepting promises of loyalty from the western Keres, Zuñi, and Hopi groups. Oñate took the oaths of the inhabitants of Acoma on October 27, 1598.[41] At that time he was completely unaware that these western Pueblos would soon shatter the tranquillity his expedition had so far enjoyed.

Chapter Two

"To Love and Fear Us"

The pueblo of Acoma stands, today as in
the sixteenth century, atop a rugged and
isolated sandstone mesa 360 feet above
the surrounding desert floor. The mesa is
massive, with two segments—a southern,
uninhabited half joined to its northern
counterpart by a narrow and treacherous
bridge of natural outcropping—covering
an area of seventy acres. Its walls are
forbidding, the smooth sandstone bluffs
not only sheer but in many places over-
hanging. Until quite recently, access to
the pueblo was gained only by way of two
pathways hidden among the crags of the
northern segment of the mesa. These
pathways are narrow, allowing passage of
only one person at a time, and in many
places consist merely of toe and finger
holes carved into the sandstone crevices.

At the summit, the pueblo itself is
arranged in wandering lines of two- and
three-story terraced adobe dwellings

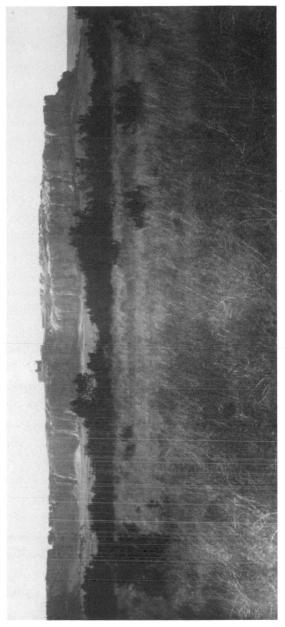

Figure 1. The pueblo of Acoma (Vernon Bailey, 1906). Photograph courtesy of the National Anthropological Archives, Smithsonian Institution, negative no. 2110-F.

whose backs face to the north, barriers against a fierce northern wind. Narrow, winding streets divide these structures, forming a veritable maze for outsiders unfamiliar with the pueblo. Adding to this complexity in Oñate's time was a network of tunnels connecting various kivas and dwellings throughout the pueblo.[1]

Water is supplied to the inhabitants of Acoma even today by rain and snow collected in large natural cisterns formed out of the sandstone bedrock. This resource, when combined with sufficient stores of the food grown on irrigated tracts of the desert below, made Acoma a virtually impregnable fortress, particularly during times of siege.[2] In their passage through the region in 1541, Coronado's men referred to the pueblo as "the greatest stronghold in the world," whose inhabitants "came down to meet us peacefully, although they could have spared themselves the trouble and stayed on their rock and we would not have been able to trouble them in the least."[3] Likewise, members of the Chamuscado-Rodríguez expedition of 1581 named Acoma "the best stronghold in existence even among Christians."[4]

This stronghold would soon test the latest Spanish arrivals. Juan de Zaldívar, maestre de campo of the expedition and nephew of Juan de Oñate, arrived at Acoma leading thirty-one men late in the afternoon of December 1, 1598. Upon his return to San Juan from an expedition to the Great Plains, Zaldívar and the soldiers under his command had received orders from Oñate to overtake the governor in the western pueblos of Zuñi. From there the maestre de campo was to accompany Oñate on his journey in search of a harbor on the South Sea, believed by the Spaniards to lie somewhere to the west. On his way to Zuñi, however, Zaldívar fell drastically short of supplies and ordered a detour to Acoma.

There he sent eight men, led by Captain Gerónimo Márquez, to follow the Acoma guides who had met the Spaniards at the base of the mesa up the narrow path to its summit. Once there, Márquez requested that wood and water be sent down to Zaldívar's camp. Although the Acomas surrendered some supplies to the Spaniards, Márquez felt the amount to be insufficient and given unwillingly. He ordered his soldiers to take several of the pueblo's leaders as hostages in order to guarantee quick delivery of the needed goods and descended with the captives to Zaldívar's camp below.

Well aware of the delicacy of the situation, Zaldívar immediately ordered the hostages released. As Márquez recounted the incident, "all he [Zaldívar] wanted was to assure the Indians that they would not be harmed or abused in any way. He thought that in this manner, as the Indians gained confidence in us, they would furnish the provisions more willingly. So he let the chiefs go." But Zaldívar's attempted diplomacy did little to instill trust in the Acomas, and the next morning representatives from the pueblo returned with only a few tortillas and three or four fanegas of maize.[5] Frustrated, the maestre de campo decided to offer hatchets and various trinkets in exchange for additional flour. Accepting the Acomas' claims that they needed two days' time to grind the requested flour, Zaldívar withdrew his camp temporarily to a watering site six miles distant.[6]

The Acomas, in the meantime, judged the Spanish demands to be too great. When Zaldívar and seventeen of his men returned to the mesa on Friday, December 4, disaster awaited them. Leaving three men below to guard the horses, Zaldívar and the fourteen others began their ascent. Again conscious of the volatile mood of the pueblo above him, the maestre de campo repeatedly "ordered

everyone to remain within sight, both soldiers and servants, in order not to molest the Indians in any way."[7] A
number of Indians met the Spaniards at the mesa's summit
and led them through its labyrinth of narrow streets, but
Zaldívar had difficulty obtaining a satisfactory amount of
flour—many Acomas pulled in the ladders to their homes,
refusing to surrender their provisions to Spanish intruders.

As the hour grew late, a now angered Zaldívar allowed
his men to separate into groups of six and proceed in
different directions, hoping to speed the gathering. Shortly
afterward, a cry broke out over the pueblo and the Spaniards found themselves attacked by the town's inhabitants
en masse. Victory was swift for the Acomas: Zaldívar, two
of his captains, eight soldiers, and two servants soon lay
dead. The few Spaniards who survived the initial fury of
the attack escaped only by hurling themselves in desperation over the mesa's edge. Those who survived landed
miraculously on sand drifts. The rest crushed themselves
on the rocks below.[8]

Upon receiving word of the deaths at Acoma, Oñate
immediately perceived the gravity of the events and opted
to return to San Juan, giving Acoma a wide berth on his
journey eastward. Upon arriving, Oñate called for a general junta on January 10, 1599, in order to decide on a proper
course of action. There, the colonists agreed on the need
for quick and effective punishment of the Indians of
Acoma. Few doubted that the assault had been premedi-
tated, with the Acomas resolving decisively to resist Spanish demands for food in the interim between Zaldívar's
request for flour on December 2 and his return to the mesa
on December 4.[9] The Spaniards who survived the incident
concurred in their testimonies regarding the affair. The
size and ferocity of the attack clearly pointed to a well-

Figure 2. "A Feast Day at Acoma" (E. S. Curtis, 1904). Photograph courtesy of the Smithsonian Institution Libraries, negative no. 91-7904.

prepared Acoma assault.[10] Caoma, a Keres native of the pueblo, later laid bare the Acoma grievance: "Because [the Spaniards] asked for such large amounts [of flour and maize], they killed them."[11]

More importantly, the European newcomers were all too cognizant that their very survival depended upon a swift and decisive reprisal against the recalcitrant Acomas. Oñate and his handful of settlers could only hope to dominate a land inhabited by what the governor estimated to be as many as sixty thousand Indians by way of intimidation. Keenly aware of the Pueblos' vast numerical superiority, Oñate realized that "the greatest force we [Spaniards] possess at present to defend our friends and ourselves is the prestige of the Spanish nation, by fear of which the Indians have been kept in check."[12]

The uprising at Acoma now gravely threatened that strategy. Upon convening the junta at San Juan, Oñate noted that the Indians were "in serious danger of revolting if the offenders [at Acoma] are not properly punished, as their vileness would be emulated by other savages."[13] Bernabé de la Casas shared Oñate's fears, claiming to have heard "many natives ask when the people of Acoma would be punished and killed. All are waiting in suspense to see what we will do."[14] Márquez likewise testified that he was "sure that if [Acoma] is not levelled and its inhabitants punished, there will be no security in all of New Mexico, nor could it be settled, as the natives of [all] the pueblos are watching what we do at Acoma and whether we punish them."[15] Clearly, the Spaniards could allow no blow to their prestige to go unpunished if they wished to remain in New Mexico. Accordingly, the junta concluded unanimously that "if these Indians were not punished . . . they would form a league, rebel, and destroy us easily."[16]

At the same time, though, Oñate astutely recognized that a careful handling of the affair could strengthen the newcomers' long-term position in New Mexico, facilitating Spanish political control and missionizing efforts. He knew that Márquez had learned "from the Indians themselves that if their [the Acomas'] crime is punished and they are not allowed to reoccupy the pueblo, it is certain that the whole land will be over-awed and it could then be settled without further difficulty."[17] Similarly, the governor realized that the manner in which the Spaniards meted out punishment to the Acomas could greatly influence the success of Franciscan efforts at converting the Pueblos to Catholicism. Oñate noted that "should they lose [their] fear [of the Spaniards] it would inevitably follow . . . that the teaching of the holy gospel would be hindered which I am under obligation to prevent."[18] But a measured response combining a powerful show of Spanish military force with a carefully orchestrated display of Franciscan compassion, the governor reasoned, might bolster the image of the friars in the eyes of their potential converts and allow the missionaries to follow safely on the heels of the military men, at Acoma and throughout the province.[19]

Eager to put his strategy into motion, Oñate appointed *sargento mayor* Vicente de Zaldívar, younger brother of the slain *maestre de campo*, to head a punitive expedition of seventy men against Acoma. The governor's instructions to the younger Zaldívar were explicit and reflected the carefully delineated roles that Oñate envisioned for both Spanish settlers and Franciscan missionaries as the key to maintaining Spanish dominance in New Mexico. Zaldívar was to offer the natives of Acoma the opportunity to surrender peacefully, but he was to proceed brutally with the conquest should that offer be rejected. Importantly, Oñate also commanded that

> if you should want to show lenience after they have been arrested, you should seek all possible means to make the Indians believe that you are doing so at the request of the friars with your forces. In this manner they will recognize the friars as their benefactors and protectors and come to love and esteem them and to fear us.[20]

The sargento mayor moved quickly to cement a place for the Spaniards in New Mexico. Zaldívar and his men arrived at the sandstone fortress of Acoma on January 21, 1599. There they found its inhabitants defiant and well prepared for the arrival of the punitive force. The Acomas had used their time well, digging holes and concealing them in the desert floor—traps set to break the legs of the Spanish mounts.[21] Upon seeing Zaldívar and his men, the pueblo's defenders

> all shouted loudly, raised their swords on high, and presented themselves in the coats of mail and other pieces of equipment they had taken from the dead Spaniards, boasting that they had killed ten Spaniards and two Mexicans, and that they [the Spaniards] were all a pack of scoundrels and whoremongers.[22]

As Gaspar Pérez de Villagrá would write ten years later, the Acomas' stance spread intimidation throughout the Spanish ranks:

> We considered the strength of the enemy, their haughty courage, emboldened by their apparent safety in their eyrie nest, the difficulties we must overcome in the ascent of the Rock, and many other things. Here we were, at least five miles from the nearest water supply. We had scarcely provisions to last us two weeks. . . . On the other hand, the savages had an abundant supply of water and provisions, so we were informed, to last them six years.[23]

The natives of Acoma rejected Zaldívar's demands that
they submit once again to European authority. On January
22, they answered his final call for surrender with a hail of
arrows that killed two of the Spaniards' horses. Zaldívar
withdrew and ordered the attack to begin at three o'clock
that afternoon.[24] Early Spanish hostilities were futile, but
as night fell Zaldívar ordered a feint on the northern bluff
while he and eleven other men scaled the southern, uninhabited section of the mesa. Successful, Zaldívar and his
men were able to hold their position through the night, and
on the morning of the twenty-third hoisted two cannons up
to their position. The fortress penetrated, Acoma soon fell.
The Spaniards turned the guns, each capable of firing two
hundred balls per volley, on the approaching natives. The
massacre was horrific, and before long the Spaniards had
won a position on the mesa's northern bluff and set fire to
the pueblo.[25]

As evening approached, the weary defenders offered to
surrender, and Zaldívar declared a cease-fire. On the
morning of the twenty-fourth the sargento mayor ordered
the leaders of the pueblo and their warriors confined to the
kivas of the village, but a skirmish soon developed that
prompted Zaldívar to order that the battle proceed without
quarter; it continued until those Acomas who remained
alive asked once again for surrender.[26]

The Spanish victory was devastating. Estimates placed
the number of Indian dead at eight hundred, while the
Spaniards numbered no dead and only a handful of
wounded.[27] Of the Indians who survived—approximately
five hundred, eighty of whom were adult males—all were
taken as prisoners and removed to San Juan, arriving there
on February 9, 1599. There they stood trial and received
convictions as rebels and as the murderers of Juan de

Zaldívar, ten Spaniards, and two servants. Oñate sentenced all males over twenty-five years of age to have one foot cut off and to be distributed among Oñate's captains and soldiers for twenty years of personal servitude. The sentences of all Acoma males between twelve and twenty-five likewise carried twenty years of servitude, as did those of all women over twelve years of age. Oñate placed girls under twelve in the charge of the father commissary, Fray Alonso Martínez, and boys of the same age group under the charge of Vicente de Zaldívar. Finally, the governor sentenced two Indians from the Hopi pueblos who were present at Acoma during the fighting to have their right hands cut off, a stern warning to the people of the far western communities.[28] Throughout the pueblos of New Mexico, few doubts remained that these European adventurers intended to stay.

Intimidation was the strategy by which Juan de Oñate had triumphantly established a Spanish presence in New Mexico in the closing years of the sixteenth century. The events at Acoma had demonstrated clearly the capabilities of Spanish military might. Those who had dared to resist Spanish will had been crushed, their people enslaved, their pueblo burned to the ground. The inhabitants of the Tompiro pueblos met a similar fate when they attempted to defy European authority in 1601.[29] It now remained for Oñate to begin the more passive process by which both Christian beliefs and a Spanish colonial structure could be grafted onto the indigenous Pueblo culture, swinging the new province into line with the rest of Spain's empire in America. As Oñate realized, this process could succeed only in places where the Indians' fear of Spanish settlers and soldiers outweighed Pueblo resistance to the Europeans' colonizing and missionary efforts.

The key to maintaining this intimidation without repeated use of arms was distance. Living among and teaching the Indians to abandon their native ways and beliefs was something to be left to the friars. Ideally, the Spanish settler was to remain separated from Pueblo culture, if not physically then psychologically, occupying the dominant, more aloof position of patriarch, judge, and punisher among the Indians. Oñate had spelled this model of dominance out clearly in his orders regarding the handling of the Acoma affair. His request for additional settlers—to boost the number of male Spaniards in the province to two hundred—was further evidence of his desire to prevent intimacy between Spanish settlers and Pueblo Indians. In a letter to the viceroy dated March 22, 1599, Oñate asked specifically for "married men, who are the solid rock on which to build a lasting new nation," to form the second wave of settlers for New Mexico.[30]

Dissent within the Spanish ranks soon threatened the continued existence of the New Mexico colony, however, thwarting the implementation of Oñate's model of Spanish dominance via distance. In the opening years of the seventeenth century, doubts about the desirability of this new land for which they had uprooted themselves and traveled so far to settle surfaced in the minds of many of the newcomers. The harshness of New Mexico's climate and the ruggedness of its environment made a forceful impact upon Oñate and his settlers, as winters proved difficult and the land sterile. For immigrants accustomed to the milder climes of central Mexico and Spain, the transition was traumatic. Desperation closely followed the disappointment that spread among the colonists as the visions of wealth and glory upon which many had staked their lives and entire fortunes in coming to New Mexico slowly gave way to full recognition of the abysmal poverty of the land

47

they now inhabited. Years of exploration had revealed neither signs of significant mineral wealth in the province nor any indication of proximity to a harbor on the South Sea to facilitate transportation and commerce to and from the colony. At the same time, tribute collected from the Pueblos was rudimentary, consisting of maize and blankets, and these in proportions insufficient to support the Spaniards and yet ruinous to the indigenous tribes.

Word of the true state of affairs in New Mexico first reached Mexico City in a letter written by Captain Luis de Velasco to the Count of Monterrey, viceroy of New Spain. The count had commissioned Velasco as an inside informant in the Oñate expedition prior to its departure in 1598, and on March 22, 1601, Velasco slipped his first report secretly into Oñate's mail bound for Mexico City.[31] In June of that year reports reached the viceroy telling of the general dissatisfaction among the colonists, particularly the 73 new settlers who had arrived to bolster Oñate's forces on December 24, 1600. Many of these latest newcomers

> complained that they had received reports, information, and letters telling of much greatness and riches, and that they had been defrauded. They claimed that they had consumed their estates and had been deprived of the tranquility they had enjoyed in New Spain; they despaired of finding enough food to eat or clothing to cover their own nakedness and that of their wives, children, and relatives.[32]

Finally, in September of 1601, while Oñate was absent on an expedition to the Great Plains, roughly two thirds of the colonists decided to risk facing charges of desertion of duty rather than remain in New Mexico. They fled the province, making their way south to Nueva Galicia with the hope of attaining viceregal protection from Oñate's wrath.[33] Once there, their condition moved Rodrigo del Río de Losa, a former governor of Nueva Galicia, to write the viceroy on January 13, 1602, and inform him that

> in what they [Oñate's men] have seen and traversed thus far they have found the land sandy and lacking in wood and water, so even if they wanted to settle it and remain in the land permanently it would not be possible, because, in addition to lacking people and silver, it lacks woods, pastures, water, and suitable land, which forced them to abandon it. Some arrived here in the province of your lordship in a pitiful condition, and it was grievous to hear those who came back tell of the plight of those who stayed behind. Your lordship should take pity on them, for their lack of clothing, food, and horses forces them to seek relief.[34]

Oñate was left with a scant handful of settlers with whom to continue the colonization of New Mexico, while over the next few years debate would rage in the royal courts of Spain and Mexico over the fate of the unfortunate colony.

In determining the future of the New Mexico settlement, policy makers in Mexico City and Madrid faced a number of difficult decisions. With gradual verification of the reports of the region's poverty came the realization that maintaining the colony would require substantial outlays from the royal treasury, an expense the crown could ill afford and one that would almost certainly fail to generate any financial return. Abandonment, however, would mean the loss of an important platform from which to launch further expansion into North America. Fray Juan de Escalona astutely summarized the dilemma in October of 1601: "Here we are at a midway point and in a position to go north or east or south [sic]. . . . In my opinion it would not be to the interest of the king to abandon this land."[35] Equally important, a withdrawal from New Mexico would remove a strategic check against any future incursions by other European colonial powers upon Spanish territory and, specifically, the rich mining country of northern Nueva Vizcaya.

Attention also had to be paid to those Indians in New Mexico who had sworn vassalage to the Spanish crown and accepted a Christian baptism. Abandoning those converts, whom Oñate numbered at six hundred in 1607,[36] could not be sanctioned for reasons of both religious conscience and political prestige. As the Count of Monterrey wrote to the king in 1602,

> It seems that a prince as Catholic and mighty as your majesty would be wholly right in not permitting us for the present to abandon what has been started, even if its maintenance should prove costly and require some expenditure from the royal treasury for the soldiers and settlers besides the expense incurred for the friars. For the discomfiture of heretics, and even of rivals of the crown of Castile who are not heretics, it is important to demonstrate clearly that we seek above all the exaltation of the faith and the extension of the holy church.[37]

With regard to the Indians themselves, Fray Francisco de Velasco argued that the fate of those Christianized Indians left behind in New Mexico would follow one of two paths: reversion to their original beliefs and religious practices, or death at the hands of those who had scorned baptism. In 1609, he wrote that

> all the hostile tribes surrounding the nations among whom the Spaniards are now settled think that the Spaniards are scoundrels and people who are concerned only with their own interests. . . . And if the hostile tribes should become aware of the danger that the peaceful tribes may be abandoned by the Spaniards, they would be confirmed in their opinion . . . and on this base their

right to start a cruel war against the whole country. . . . Although savages, they [the Christian Indians] implore your majesty not to leave them in a situation in which, having abandoned their faith for ours, they would be in danger of being slaughtered.[38]

Transplanting the newly converted Indians to lands in New Spain was also unfeasible since none of them would willingly forsake their homeland on behalf of their new-found religion. According to Velasco, any attempts by colonial officials to force the relocation of the baptized Indians would almost certainly fail because "the roughness of the country is so great that it would prove impossible to carry out this removal."[39] Indeed, in 1601 a rumor that the Spaniards were thinking of deserting the colony and ex-tracting all natives who professed Christianity had report-edly led to panic in San Juan among a large group of local Indian servants and Acoma slaves who had recently ac-cepted baptism, sending them running for the shelter of the countryside.[40]

Such fears on the part of the Pueblos, in Oñate's opin-ion of August 24, 1607, could also endanger those Span-iards leaving New Mexico and, more importantly, jeopar-dize any future attempts at resettlement and conversion. He predicted that any attempt to remove the baptized Indians forcibly would result in

> not only that holy baptism will be refused in these lands at all times, but the natives will not even dare to welcome the Spaniards in future years if their children, brothers, and relatives are taken away. . . . This [removal] will no doubt give rise to many difficulties and dangers, for, at the time of their removal, the land will rise and take arms to prevent it . . . for even though they may not be natu-rally war-like, they would become bold on seeing how few of us are left for this task.[41]

51

Reluctantly, Viceroy Luis de Velasco made the final decision to maintain the province of New Mexico on January 29, 1609.[42] Oñate's resignation as governor, given in the face of controversy over his misrepresentation of conditions in New Mexico in his early reports and his harsh actions in dealing with the participants in the Acoma uprising, had been accepted by the viceroy on February 27, 1608. Oñate, however, had been forbidden to leave the province pending the decision as to the fate of its remaining colonists.[43] But like Oñate, Velasco recognized that maintaining Spanish dominance in New Mexico with so few settlers amid such a large native population hinged upon the preservation of an image of Spanish superiority that outweighed any numerical advantage on the part of the Pueblos. On March 30, 1609, he appointed don Pedro de Peralta governor and captain general of the province of New Mexico with orders to hold the territory and "maintain and enhance the prestige of the Spaniards among the natives."[44] Those settlers who remained in the province would be allowed to continue their existence in that remote corner of the empire. For Oñate, his dream of a "new world, greater than New Spain,"[45] had vanished. In its place now stood a barren and impoverished colony, a handful of Spaniards, and an overwhelming Pueblo majority.

Part II

Weathering the Storm

Pueblo Cultural Endurance

Throughout the seventeenth century, Pueblo culture and tradition remained strong in the face of Spanish political domination and intense missionizing efforts in New Mexico. Although the arrival of Juan de Oñate and his settlers in 1598 injected turmoil into Pueblo society sufficient to make Indian conversion to Christianity a practical and even widespread phenomenon, such conversions did not necessarily signify the complete renunciation of established Pueblo beliefs and practices. On the contrary, a numerically small Spanish presence in the land made possible the preservation and continued following of the old ways.

Because church doctrine and Spanish colonial law forbade many acts of cultural preservation, the Indians kept them hidden from the eyes of Spanish overlords. At times, conflict within the Hispanic community tempered the zeal with which Franciscan missionaries and civil authorities enforced restrictions on traditional native practices. Such disagreements opened up opportunities for some Pueblos to play opposing factions off one another in a calculated effort to regain the freedoms lost at the close of the previous century.

The Spanish entrada profoundly disrupted established trade and agricultural patterns in the region, jeopardizing the means by which a sizable native population had sustained itself for centuries in a land of scarce resources. The newcomers quickly took control of Pueblo food sources and consequently damaged relations between these sedentary farmers and the surrounding nomadic Athapaskan groups. As hunger and the threat of Apache and Navajo depredations gnawed at those pueblos held most tightly in the Spaniards' grip, acceptance of Christian baptism—with its accompanying access to mission food stores and Spanish military protection—became the most viable option for survival for all but the most stalwart opponents of the new faith.

Still, in many instances Pueblo renunciation of traditional beliefs in favor of Christian doctrine was far from complete. As the dust of the initial military conquest slowly settled, Pueblo resistance to the demands of their new overlords continued, shifting from the battlefield to the altars and confessionals of the newly built churches and behind the closed doors of native ceremonial chambers. Close scrutiny of the surviving documentary evidence brings to light this clandestine aspect of Pueblo cultural preservation and refutes the classic interpretation—put forward by Paul Horgan and others—of Pueblo-Spanish cultural interaction as one of complete native submission to the perceived superiority of a new faith promoted by European military might.[1]

At the same time, the evidence challenges more recent arguments by Edward Spicer, Van Hastings Garner, and a host of other scholars that sufficient flexibility existed in both Pueblo and Catholic religious practices on a day-to-day level to foster a gradual fusion of the two belief systems, yielding an amalgamated faith quite different from either of the two originals.[2] This syncretic school of thought is grounded heavily in contemporary observation of folk-Catholicism and Pueblo ceremony as practiced in present-day New Mexico. Such a perspective ignores the fact that, regardless of these long-term trends, for the better part of the seventeenth century serious punishments awaited baptized Pueblos caught practicing traditional rites by watchful friars. Exploiting opportunities to engage in traditional ceremonies and practices behind a facade of Christian piety thus took on a deadly seriousness for those dedicated to preserving the old ways.

Throughout the pre-revolt period in New Mexico, dissension within the Hispanic community provided many such opportunities for Pueblo traditionalists. Perhaps no division aided the Pueblo cause more than the long-running conflict that smoldered between colonial church and state. Much like the royal officials called upon to arbitrate disputes between secular and clerical authorities in seventeenth-century New Mexico, twentieth-century historians have pored over hundreds of surviving decrees, denunciations, and depositions in an effort to determine which side, church or state, spoke most truthfully in its accusations against the other. Several authors have approached this issue by dividing the Hispanic community into three camps—Franciscan missionaries, bureaucratic authorities appointed by the crown, and permanent settlers—and focusing on the fractures within and the ultimate balance of power among these three interest groups.[3]

In doing so, these scholars have largely neglected the

people who stood to gain most from the tensions between church and state in New Mexico—the Pueblo Indians. Even France V. Scholes, in his otherwise masterful works on the frictions between secular and clerical powers in the province, adopted a somewhat patronizing and superficial stance with regard to this important aspect of the conflict. The bitter antagonism between civil and ecclesiastical authorities during the seventeenth century, according to Scholes, "had a most demoralizing effect on the Indians, who had little understanding of the issues at stake."[4]

The extant documentation from the period (much of it recovered by Scholes himself) argues to the contrary. Many Pueblos proved quite adept at recognizing the significance of strife within the Hispanic community and manipulating events to their own advantage. In the process, they exhibited a Pueblo heritage with the strength to weather more than three generations of Spanish rule in the seventeenth century, and the patience to await the day when New Mexico would be returned to the hands of its oldest inhabitants.

to the probable amusement of their native parishioners, since the days of Eulate's administration. There can be little doubt that incidents like these seriously damaged Franciscan prestige in the eyes of a significant number of the Pueblo converts to Christianity, injecting renewed vigor into native efforts to preserve and practice the old ways in preference to the new.

For the Pueblos, Rosas's economic ventures and his scorn for the clergy opened prospects for religious freedom of a kind not seen since the time of Eulate. The Tano inhabitants of Pecos, for instance, traded their labor for a pledge from Rosas not to interfere in their traditional ceremonies. Throughout the latter half of 1638 and up until 1641, Rosas's opponents repeatedly denounced the governor for, as Francisco Salazar testified, striking a deal with "the Indian captains of the pueblo of Pecos to bring him blankets and hides . . . [in exchange for which] he would allow them to name their [own] captains as they had in antiquity, the captains which carry out the idolatry."[34]

In late December 1639, the Indians of Taos rebelled against the Franciscans in their pueblo, desecrating the church and killing Fray Pedro de Miranda, the guardian of the convent there, along with two other Spaniards. They then moved on to Picurís with the intent of killing the friar in residence there. Warned of his impending fate, the friar fled to San Ildefonso, thereby escaping death. Critics blamed Rosas for the uprising, claiming that his policy of nativism had encouraged the Indians of Taos to revolt and pointing to his decision to delay dispatching a punitive expedition to the pueblo as proof of his collusion with the rebels.[35]

Rosas's administration exerted an unquestionable influence on those Pueblos who chose to resist European efforts to erase their heritage. Unfortunately, gaps in the historical record prevent any meaningful interpretation of Pueblo benefits from the strife between civil and clerical authorities during the tenures of New Mexico's next six Spanish governors. The arrival of Governor Bernardo López de Mendizábal in July 1659, however, opened a new and well-documented chapter in the struggle between church and state in the province. His administration would spark a chain of events leading to the most dramatic and open displays of Pueblo cultural heritage since the days before the arrival of Juan de Oñate at the close of the previous century.

Little survives to tell the story of López de Mendizábal's early life. The son of Captain Cristóbal López de Mendizábal, a Spaniard, and doña Leona de Pastrana, a criolla, he was born in the province of Chietla, Mexico, around 1620. In his early years he studied arts and canon law at the Jesuit colleges in Puebla and Mexico City and at the Royal University of Mexico. After a short period of service as a soldier, he resumed the habit and took the minor orders. Though he meant to continue on to major orders, his family prevented him from proceeding, for reasons unknown. Consequently, López de Mendizábal chose to return to a career in the military, serving at various times and locations as soldier, judge, and governor. In South America he was stationed for a time at the presidio of Cartagena and also served in the *galleon armada*. In Mexico he held, at times unknown, the offices of alcalde mayor and capitán á guerra. In 1658, the viceroy appointed him governor of New Mexico, and he made ready to leave for that province with the convoy of the winter of 1658–59.[36]

Once in power, López de Mendizábal engaged in the usual corruptions and exploitation of indigenous labor. He was active in the slave trade, organizing hunting expeditions into Apache country and shipping captives for sale in the markets of El Parral, seven hundred miles to the south.[37] In another venture, he employed Indians from Taos and Picurís to build carts and wagons in which he shipped salt, piñon, and hides, gathered for him by Indian laborers in the district of Las Salinas, to El Parral in the summer of 1659. But López de Mendizábal made no arrangements for the return of the Indian drivers, leaving them stranded far from home.[38] At the same time, he issued an auto prohibiting all unauthorized export of tradable goods out of New Mexico. He justified the move as necessary to sustain the province, which had just come through a period of famine,[39] but general accusation pointed to the act as a protection of his trade in El Parral.[40] In his first months in office, López de Mendizábal had taken bold steps toward making his tenure in New Mexico a profitable one.

Like many of his predecessors, the governor recognized that access to Pueblo labor was a key to economic success — a key closely guarded by members of the clergy and the permanent settlers of the Hispanic community. Accordingly, he initiated a number of policy changes early in his administration that were designed to break this stranglehold over the native work force. One of his first acts was to double the wage for Indian labor in the province established by the Royal Order of 1620. In addition to daily meals, workers would now receive the equivalent of one full rather than one-half real in cloth, antelope skins, corn, or wool per day. He justified the act by citing common knowledge "of the tyranny with which the Indians of [New Mexico] were generally used," but an outcry among the Hispanic settlers was inevitable.[41]

López de Mendizábal took a direct approach in his efforts to pry Pueblo workers from the control of the Franciscan missionaries. He clearly resented the clergy's monopoly over labor in those pueblos in which missions were located, as evidenced in a letter from the governor to Fray Diego de Santander dated July 20, 1660. In response to Santander's charges that he was not cooperating in the effort to Christianize the Pueblos, López de Mendizábal replied that although he did not know the extent to which the Indians understood the Christian faith, he was quite sure that they did know how "to guard and herd an infinite number of livestock, to serve as slaves, and to fill barns with grain, cultivated and harvested with their own blood, not for their humble homes, but for those of the friars."[42] Later, the governor would offer his opinion that "it cannot be to the interest of divine worship . . . that [the friars] should keep the Indians in dungeons and work-shops weaving frieze and sackcloth to be sold there and sent to other provinces [for which] they maintain the shops right in the convents."[43]

To remedy the situation, López de Mendizábal enacted strict new regulations in the later part of 1659 that limited the services the Pueblos could provide for the missions. Except for servants essential to the operation of the church, Indians in the missions would no longer be exempt from tribute payments. Henceforth, only a *cantor mayor* and a sacristan could serve members of the clergy. All other workers in the missions had either to volunteer their efforts or collect the newly defined general wage from the church. Strict enforcement of this proclamation exempted the Indians from performing even the simplest services on the friars' behalf. The Franciscans soon found themselves deprived of the herdsmen, translators, cooks, porters, harvesters, and others so crucial to the smooth operation of the missions.[44]

Choosing his lieutenants carefully, López de Mendizábal saw to it that his decrees were carried out to the letter. In the Salinas pueblos, for example, the governor handpicked Nicolás de Aguilar, a mestizo, as his alcalde mayor for the district. According to Miguel de Noriega, López de Mendizábal's secretary of government and war, the governor put Aguilar "into that position purposely to deal with the religious as they deserved, and had removed from it Captain Pedro de Leiva because he was partial to the affairs of the church."[45] Aguilar was not a holy man. A reputed criminal who had fled northward into New Mexico after killing an uncle in El Parral, Aguilar enforced López de Mendizábal's policies with a brutality that won him the title "Atila" in clerical circles.[46] Juan Domínguez de Mendoza, whom members of the clergy characterized as "a man conspicuously inimical to the ecclesiastics," served as López de Mendizábal's lieutenant governor, the acting civil authority for the entire Río Abajo region of New Mexico.[47] Members of the clergy and their supporters would later accuse both men of injecting deliberate malice and humiliation into their treatment of the missionaries as they supervised the governor's reforms in the pueblos under their respective jurisdictions.[48]

While some Pueblos accepted release from service to the missions only to find themselves pressed into labor on projects of the governor's design, others surely benefited from his policies. López de Mendizábal clearly held little respect for the Franciscans in New Mexico, and his indiscriminate persecution of the missionaries once again provided opportunities for discontented native parishioners to vent their frustrations with members of the clergy. The governor's words toward the friars were unremittingly harsh; to him, the religious of New Mexico were at best "drunken fools."[49] With the Indians alertly watching, López de Mendizábal incessantly challenged ecclesiastical authority in the province. In June 1660, Fray Miguel de Sacristán, minister at Santa Fe, claimed that López de Mendizábal dared "to say to the very religious themselves that there is no other head here than the governor. He said to certain heathen who came with others who are Christians to talk to him, that there was none here to be recognized save himself and God."[50]

Traditionally, the governor of New Mexico periodically toured the pueblos in the province, assembling the inhabitants and listening to their complaints and disputes. Critics accused López de Mendizábal of focusing these proceedings on the wrongdoings of the clergy and using the opportunity to make scathing inquisitions into the day-to-day practices of the friars. Sacristán, in his letter to the custodian of June 16, 1660, recorded his fear that his parishioners, "miserable Indians who are without capacity," might use these proceedings to make slanderous accusations against their pastors, becoming wildly inflated by such novel power over the prelates.[51]

During one of these sessions in the pueblo of Alamillo, López de Mendizábal listened to the accusations of a native woman against the resident friar, a man ninety years old, claiming that the priest had engaged in sexual relations with her and then denied the woman a prearranged payment. The governor forced the friar to pay the woman her claims, an event that caused "all the Indians of that pueblo, both men and women, and other persons who went with [López de Mendizábal] and saw the circumstance, to laugh immoderately, as if ridiculing the minister."[52] (López de

Mendizábal later explained that it had not been his intention to humiliate the priest. He had simply misunderstood the interpreter present at the scene, thinking that the woman had accused an elderly native in the pueblo. He then asked the friar to give the woman an antelope skin in order to placate her and continued with the proceedings.)[53]

For many Pueblos, these hearings doubtlessly provided an all-too-rare opportunity to denounce publicly the misconduct of the clerics who lived among them. Accounts of friars abusing the Indians over whom they ministered are strewn throughout the documents of the period, ranging from complaints against excessive corporal punishment to the tale of friars Velasco and Guerra in the Zuñi pueblos. In 1655, angered at a group of Indians who had lodged complaints with the governor regarding conditions in the missions, Guerra

> had [the Indians] brought to him, and he went to their homes to search them. He found some feathers or idols, and consequently seized [the people] and ordered turpentine brought so as to set fire to them. . . . One of them he [Guerra] sent to his [the witness's] pueblo. The Indian was about to die of his burns and could not walk.[54]

The victim soon died, and although Guerra and Velasco were held in Santa Fe for investigation for an unknown period of time, both were back in the missions by the time of López de Mendizábal's administration.

Many Pueblos also complained of sexual abuse by members of the clergy. Upon his arrival in Santa Fe, López de Mendizábal was informed by the sargento mayor, Francisco Gómez, that "he knew many women who told him that they did not go to confession because they were solicited in the confessional."[55] Rumor held Fray Diego de Parraga, one of the ministers at Tajique at this time, to have

107

had sex with as many as forty of his parishioners. The friar himself eventually confessed to fathering a child by a married Indian woman.[56] The governor himself told the story of the arrest of Fray Luis Martínez

> for this friar having committed the execrable crime of forcing a woman, cutting her throat, and burying her in an office, or cell, in the *convento* of Los Taos. [López de Mendizábal] reported the case to the prelate and asked him to take proper measures, lest Fray Luis Martínez commit another crime, he having returned to those pueblos, or lest the Indians there should kill him and revolt, as they did on another occasion because of an event like this. . . . The investigation . . . of the case was made at the request of the Indians; for Fray Juan Lobato had buried the body of the dead woman in the church, having taken it from the cell, or office, secretly so that it might not be known.[57]

In the summer of 1660, the dispute over the governor's right to conduct these inquiries erupted, and the ensuing events soon loosened the Franciscans' hold over their Pueblo parishioners even further. In June, controversy arose over the alleged sexual misconduct of Fray Diego de Parraga. An Indian from Tajique, Francisco Nieto, had approached López de Mendizábal and informed him that Parraga "kept taking his wife away from him at night to sleep with her, and that he had had a daughter by her, and that this had been going on for a period of three years."[58] The governor sent Aguilar to bring the woman to Santa Fe. Upon learning of this, Parraga confessed to the charges, saying "that it was the truth, that he had gone there one night to see the girl, who was his daughter, such were his sins, and . . . as a man he had enjoyed the woman carnally."[59]

An investigation quickly followed, presided over by the

custodian of New Mexico, Fray García de San Francisco, since the matter fell under ecclesiastical jurisdiction. Aguilar and Esteban Clemente, the Indian governor of Las Salinas, were ordered to collect the women who had complaints against Parraga—twenty-two of them in all—and assemble them in Tajique. When Aguilar presented the witnesses for examination, San Francisco accused him of making his own interrogation of the women, thereby tampering in an ecclesiastical investigation, and excommunicated Nicolás de Aguilar on the spot.[60]

López de Mendizábal's reaction was immediate. On June 12 he issued an auto denying the jurisdiction of the custodian as an ordinary ecclesiastical judge, a power usually granted only to those of episcopal status. "And on the contrary," López wrote, "he is to abstain from everything not connected with the administration of the holy sacraments and that which pertains thereto."[61] This order in effect denied San Francisco the power of excommunication and so deprived the church in New Mexico of one of its most powerful weapons. The blow was an effective one. Any threats of excommunication that San Francisco might make against López de Mendizábal or anyone else in the province were for the time being rendered impotent, the governor having made it clear that the custodian's authority as ecclesiastical judge was based precariously upon tradition.

By the end of the month, López de Mendizábal's persecution had begun to take its toll, as friars started to abandon the missions and their Pueblo parishioners. Fray Antonio Aguado resigned his post at Abó, ostensibly because of Aguilar's denying him the use of his Tompiro translator.[62] Meanwhile, San Francisco drafted a letter to the viceroy in Mexico City expressing the collective view of

109

the friars "that if they did not receive relief from this [Mexico] city they would have to consume the Holy Sacrament of all their churches and depart from the Kingdom."[63]

But relief was necessarily slow in coming, and as López de Mendizábal continued his policies, "through these rigorous acts the ministers were perishing, so that by twos and threes they were being obliged to desert their *doctrinas*, as did Fathers Diego de Barragán, Nicolás de Freitas, Fray Antonio, and Fray Fernando de Velasco."[64] In all, six friars resigned their missions, four of them in the Las Salinas district alone. Dismayed, the friars watched as support for the missions disappeared and attendance at mass plummeted. (Many accused the governor of issuing direct orders for the services to be boycotted.)[65] As Fray Nicolás de Freitas wrote, "it got to such a pass that they [the religious] received no obvention of any kind, neither for marriages, burials, watch services, festivals for patron saints, nor for anything else."[66]

Meanwhile, emboldened by the highly visible anticlerical stance of this latest governor, representatives of the inhabitants of Tesuque approached López de Mendizábal at the *villa real* in Santa Fe and asked him to lift the official ban on the dancing of the kachinas. The Franciscans in New Mexico had targeted these traditional Pueblo dances for eradication—with varying degrees of success—since the earliest days of colonization. In the minds of the friars, the dances embodied all of what they considered to be the hedonistic spirit of the Pueblos from the time before the conquest, full of idolatry, devil worship, and sexual excess, even incest. Fray Nicolás de Freitas provided one of the more provocative Franciscan interpretations of two of the many varieties of the dance, quoted here at length:

Prior to performing the first variety of this dance, the Indians fast two or three days, and after the fast is ended comes the day of the dance, when the naked dancers put on their faces a kind of hood or mask, with a small hole through which they can see a little; these masks are made of cloth or buckskin; and they also put on other masks, dyed black. Those who wear these are the most idolatrous. Before they come out in public they practice in their underground council chambers [kivas], and when they come out in public one of them puts the offerings . . . in the place where the dance is to be performed. The other dancers perform the dance around the offering. The language used is a tongue which is not understood, even by the Indians themselves, or at least they are unwilling to say more than that it is the language of the devil. If they are asked for what purpose they perform these dances, they say that it is to obtain the woman they desire, and that the devil will give her to them, or, that he will give them corn, or any other thing that they request. One or more of them seize small palm leaves, and cruelly beat until they bleed one or more of the dancers who desire to make that sort of blood sacrifice to the devil; they all become so frenzied that they seem to be beside themselves without having previously taken any liquor whatever which might intoxicate them. Sometimes they leave this dance and enter any house which they care to, and enjoy the woman who seems pleasing to them.

In the second variety of the dance there is no fasting; sometimes there is the ritualistic performance already mentioned, but always with the masks on. This ceremony has less solemnity but much superstition, in which fathers have intercourse with daughters, sons with mothers, and brothers with sisters, no attention being paid to relationship.[67]

López de Mendizábal was aware of the controversial nature of the dances and the fact that many of them held religious significance for those who danced them. As

111

Cristóbal Anaya would later testify: "It was impossible that he could fail to know it, for everyone else in the kingdom, especially the criollos like himself, knew it was and said so."[68] Nevertheless, the governor ordered that the delegation from Tesuque perform the dance before him. López de Mendizábal's interpretation of the display stands in marked contrast to that of Nicolás de Freitas:

> It was simply an exhibition of agility. . . . Ten or twelve Indians dressed themselves in the ordinary clothes which they commonly wear and put on masks painted with human figures of men; then half of them, with timbrels, such as are commonly used in New Spain, in their hands, went out to the plaza. The others carried thongs, or whips, in their hands. They placed in the middle of the plaza four to six watermelons; . . . after putting the watermelons in the middle of the plaza, those who were dancing continued to do so noisily, sounding the timbrels crazily, as they are accustomed to do, and saying, "Hu, hu, hu." In this fashion they circled around the plaza and the other Indians with the thongs went along, leaping, watching the watermelons, or prizes, from a distance, and allowing opportunity for other youths and boys, Indians or others, to slip in and snatch the watermelons. The one who did they chased, and if they caught him they gave him many blows with the thongs, but if they did not catch him, he, being more fleet of foot, carried off the watermelon without receiving any lashes. When several had thus run away the dance stopped.[69]

The governor later acknowledged knowing that this was but one of many variations of the kachina ceremony as danced by the different language groups among the Pueblos, and he admitted harboring suspicions about whether or not this display was truly representative of the dances he was being asked to permit. Nevertheless, López de Mendizábal pronounced the dances "mere foolishness on the part of the Indians, an entertainment," and granted general permission for them to be performed. He stipulated only that the dances could not be performed within the kivas. Instead, they were to be danced above ground, where they could be openly observed.[70]

The proclamation caused considerable concern among many members of the Hispanic community, and the governor could not have failed to notice the reactions of the settlers gathered in the villa who heard him give the first order for the kachinas to be danced. Certainly Thomé Domínguez de Mendoza had noticed, for he "knew from the faces of those who were present that they were much affected by this action, but offered no opposition to it because the speaker was their governor and captain general."[71]

Dancing quickly erupted across the province. Dismayed, the friars reported the resurrection of the kachinas in Cuarac and all the pueblos of Las Salinas, in Alameda, Nambé, Cochití, and others.[72] By January of 1661, rumors had spread through the pueblos telling of a very old man who had sent word to the Indians of Cuarac that they should come out and receive him, and that they should bring him a woman of their own choosing. They brought him a mestizo woman

> who lives like an Indian in the pueblo who was very much adorned. They asked the old man who he was, for they did not know him. He said to them: "Don't you know me? I am not surprised, for you have kept me in exile for so many years, but now I am coming back because you are now living as I desire; now I am going to be happy among you."[73]

For this ancient holy man, as for medicine men throughout the pueblos, López de Mendizábal's corrosive challenge to

Deer dance of The Indori Indians at Santa Fe - N. M. 1883.

Figure 5. Dancers in the plaza of Santa Fe (Christian Barthelmess, 1883). Photograph courtesy of the National Anthropological Archives, Smithsonian Institution, negative no. 56,958.

the clergy had signaled a time to return from exile. The Indians took the old man through the pueblo at night and danced in the underground kiva until dawn.[74]

The friars were powerless to stop the kachinas. In Isleta, during one of the dances, Fray Salvador de Guerra, "not being able to restrain them . . . went through the pueblo with a cross upon his shoulders, a crown of thorns, and a rope about his neck, beating his naked body, in order that they might stop the dance."[75] Unfortunately for Guerra and the church of New Mexico, the effort was in vain. Expressing the anguish of the friars, Fray Francisco de Salazar of Senecú wrote that the Indians "are totally lost, without faith, without law, and without devotion to the church; they neither respect nor obey their ministers, and it makes one weep to see that in such a short time they have lost and forgotten what they have been taught in all these years."[76]

But the Pueblos' celebration of cultural revival was to be short-lived. In the spring of 1661 the friars' cries for help were answered when a convoy from Mexico City arrived at last, bringing with it a new commissary of the Holy Office, Fray Alonzo de Posadas. The arm of Spanish ecclesiastical authority was soon felt again throughout northern New Mexico. A new governor for the province, Diego de Peñalosa, arrived in August of the same year. With the authority of the Inquisition and the support of the new governor behind him, Posadas immediately reinstated the ban on the kachinas and ordered all masks and costumes connected with the dances to be collected and handed over to him.[77] Posadas also began strictly enforcing Indian attendance at church services, and in November 1661 Peñalosa overturned López de Mendizábal's decree limiting each mission to two servants exempt from tribute.[78]

115

Aware of the fate that awaited them, many of López de Mendizábal's lieutenants prepared to flee the province. On the night of April 30, 1662, they were intercepted at Isleta, carrying with them all the payments of tribute from the pueblo of Acoma. Posadas arrested four of them, Diego Romero, Cristóbal de Anaya Almazán, Francisco Gómez, and Nicolás de Aguilar. Two others escaped with the tribute and the horses of the other four.[79] López de Mendizábal's arrest soon followed, and the accused were held in Santa Fe pending a judicial review of López de Mendizábal's actions as governor by his successor and the approach of cool weather. In October, a convoy formed, and the prisoners were shipped to Mexico City to stand trial before the Inquisition.[80] Upon his arrival in Mexico City on April 28, 1663, the ex-governor was immediately confined to a cell in the secret prisons of the Inquisition to await trial. He would spend the next year and a half in that cell, grow ill, call for a confessor, and die there on September 16, 1664.[81]

On the eve of his death, Bernardo López de Mendizábal could look back and reflect on an administration that had, for whatever purpose, taken significant steps toward destroying Spanish authority among the Pueblos. In three years he had managed to untie much of what had strung Pueblo-Hispanic society together, however loosely, for sixty years, making a mockery of the church and its friars in the eyes of its recent converts. For the Pueblos, almost sixty years of careful cultural preservation had come close to fruition, for they had tasted freedom as it had not existed among their people for more than two generations. Only one obstacle—the physical presence of Spaniards—remained to be surmounted before a return to life as it was before the coming of Oñate could be complete.

Henceforth, though, the Pueblos would not be aided by conflict between church and state. Although relations between Peñalosa and the clergy were nearly as tempestuous as those in the days of López de Mendizábal, disputes between the new governor and the Franciscans centered on questions of Peñalosa's corruption and the issue of ecclesiastical authority. For the most part, Peñalosa declined to interfere with Posada's conservative Indian policies.[82] Over the next decade and a half, as threats to the security of the region became more acute, those policies became increasingly repressive. And as the Pueblos found fewer and fewer venues through which to preserve and practice their traditional ways, the pressures for revolt increased and slowly percolated to the surface.

Part III

A Dissolving Presence

The Disintegration of European Authority in
Seventeenth-Century New Mexico

While Pueblo culture maintained its strength over the
course of the seventeenth century, the mainstays of Spanish
authority in the region slowly eroded. In the years following Oñate's initial colonization, events gradually isolated
the province from the mainstream of Spanish-American
society to the south, and the flow of immigrants into the
region slowed to a trickle. Those Spaniards who remained
in New Mexico found themselves and their descendants
trapped in a cross-acculturative process with the land's
native inhabitants that over the next three-quarters of a
century would blur the outlines of Spanish culture, closing
the gap between European settler and Pueblo Indian.
Three generations after Oñate had called upon his fellow
Spaniards to maintain sovereignty by distancing themselves from the surrounding Indian populace, little remained of his strategy. As this distance that Oñate had seen
as critical diminished, the mystique of Spanish omnipo-

tence that underscored European colonial authority in the region fell into jeopardy.

Physical and economic barriers severed New Mexico's Hispanic population from administrative, commercial, and cultural developments in the more cosmopolitan parts of the viceroyalty. Forbidding terrain, wildly unpredictable weather, and depredations by nomadic Indians on New Spain's far northern frontier made travel on the long route linking Mexico City and Santa Fe hazardous and only infrequently attempted. Royal officials initiated a convoy system of transport to and from the northern province, but bureaucratic inefficiency and almost incessant bickering between competing interests over the right to own and operate the system ensured that service to New Mexico was sporadic at best.

Cut off for the most part from the flow of commerce and immigrants churning to the south, New Mexico's settlers could not escape almost total immersion in the ways and beliefs of the land's overwhelming Pueblo majority. Surviving documents offer glimpses into this process of acculturation that slowly obscured the ethnic and cultural distinctions between Pueblo and Hispanic worlds. Miscegenation, a force of change as powerful as it was inevitable almost from the moment of inception of the northern colony, quickly undercut any hopes Oñate may have held for European dominance based on physical separation of the two peoples and the distinctiveness of Spanish society. Over the next three generations, people of mixed Pueblo and Spanish ancestry changed the nature of New Mexican society profoundly, not only by serving as one of several conduits for the exchange of beliefs and practices between the two heritages but also by challenging the norms and limitations of a caste-conscious Spanish colonial system.

As these changes clouded the outlines of Spanish authority in New Mexico, Pueblo society suffered unremittingly from famine and epidemic diseases, the labor and tribute demands of colonial overlords, and the hostilities of surrounding Athapaskans. By the latter half of the 1660s these factors had rendered life under the Spanish yoke unbearable to a growing majority of the region's native populace. Many Pueblos turned to the concept of a coordinated show of force as a plausible means of ridding the land of its nonaboriginal inhabitants. But rivalries between Pueblo language groups, as well as divisions within individual communities separating those who still reaped benefits from allegiance to church and colonial authorities from those who advocated complete renunciation of the Spanish way, placed serious obstacles in the way of leaders struggling to plan a region-wide revolt.[1] More than one attempt fell victim to the apathy of a rival Pueblo group or, worse, the treachery of informants with Hispanic sympathies. Yet as the situation continued to deteriorate for New Mexico's Pueblo peoples, the call to rebel would gain unprecedented support and culminate in the events of August 1680.

Chapter Six

A Forgotten Province

Following the decision in 1609 by Spanish colonial officials to maintain the
province, the colony of New Mexico slowly withdrew from the mainstream of Spanish-American commerce and migration
and faded from the foremost thoughts of
officials in Mexico City and Madrid.
Physically, the province's isolation was
virtually complete. Fifteen hundred
miles separated Santa Fe from Mexico
City, a six-month journey for those traveling between Spain's northernmost outpost and the viceregal capital. The route
to New Mexico from the interior of New
Spain passed first along the more heavily
traveled road from Mexico City to
Zacatecas. From there smaller roads
continued on to the mining settlements
of Nueva Vizcaya's far northern frontier.
The most remote of these, Santa Bárbara, gave travelers bound for Santa Fe a
final opportunity to rest, stock up on

supplies, and soak in what few trappings of European civilization the mining town had to offer before embarking on the arduous 750-mile journey to New Mexico's remote provincial capital.

From the time of Oñate until the end of the colonial period, this northern stretch of the camino real passed through territory reputed to be some of the most forbidding in the New World.[1] From the mining camps at Santa Bárbara, the route briefly followed tributaries of the Río Conchos northeast before turning directly north to cross the harsh desert terrain of the Mesa Central, which extends across the present-day state of Chihuahua. As it approached to within a hundred miles of the Río del Norte (now the Río Grande), the trail split. Those traveling by foot, on horseback, or with light wagons continued north, weaving through the mountainous sand dunes at Samalayuca and fording the Río del Norte at a point just west of present-day El Paso. Heavier wagons followed an alternative course, moving northeast to skirt the edge of the dunes and then turning northwest to follow the banks of the Río del Norte up the El Paso valley to the same crossing point.

While the crossing of the Río del Norte marked official entry into the province of New Mexico, the worst of the journey still lay ahead. Once across the river, the route continued northward along its banks for a distance of about seventy miles. There, the smooth banks of the Río del Norte gave way to more rugged terrain as the river wound its way through the foothills of the Black Mountains to the west and the Caballo and Fray Cristóbal ranges to the east. Imposing mesas broken only by intricate networks of arroyos—deep, dry canyons prone to flash flooding during the unpredictable bouts of rainfall in the region—abutted the river, rendering its banks impassable. This landscape

123

forced travelers to leave the river for a ninety-mile journey across the hostile desert basin aptly named by early explorers the Jornada del Muerto.² From there the trail joined the river once again, passing through the southernmost Piro pueblos and continuing into the heart of the Pueblo-dominated region of northern New Mexico, arriving at last at Santa Fe.

Difficult topography was only one obstacle confronting would-be travelers to the northern province. Weather patterns in the region made life hard on those who chose to journey across the hostile terrain. Blistering desert temperatures combined with scarcity of water beyond the banks of the land's few rivers to make travel during the summer months extremely hazardous. With spring came seasonal dust storms. High winds and biting sands could erupt with almost no warning, cutting visibility to a matter of yards within minutes, scattering people and livestock, and withdrawing just as suddenly, leaving those caught in their path to agonize over the resultant damage and disarray. Spring also thawed mountain snows that often flooded the river basins, making crossings dangerous if not impossible. This hazard reappeared in late summer, when the area experienced its short but at times torrential seasonal rains.³

And not least, Europeans who journeyed between Nueva Vizcaya and New Mexico in the seventeenth century risked falling victim to the hostilities of any one of the several nomadic Indian groups who populated the lands through which the route passed. According to one traveler, Fray Alonso de Benavides, the trail north from Santa Bárbara exposed its followers to "very great risk, because the route passes through the territory inhabited by the Tobosos, Tarahumares, Tepeoanes, Sumas, Hanos and other very ferocious, barbarous and indomitable tribes."⁴

124

The threat forced Europeans to travel only with an armed escort. Even then, cunning and subterfuge were often required for successful passage through hostile lands:

> Whenever we go through their lands, if they see we are few in number, they attack us face to face and do all the damage they can. For this reason it is impossible to pass there with fewer than twelve men on horseback, all very well armed. Even then, it is necessary to proceed cautiously; and in the early part of the night a fire is lighted somewhere to divert their attention, while we advance as far as possible beyond it. Even when they see a large force, they lie in ambush by night and at least do whatever harm they can to the horses.[5]

Farther north the threat persisted, as potential raids by bands of Mescalero and, possibly, Chiricahua Apaches added to the worries of those passing through the Jornada del Muerto.

Given the dangers of passage between New Spain and Santa Fe, settlers, Franciscans, and royal officials alike quickly recognized that the route could be traversed safely only by large, heavily armed groups. Accordingly, a convoy system arose in the early years of the seventeenth century that soon became the lifeline by which the northern province maintained its ties to the rest of the viceroyalty. Because their decision to maintain a Spanish presence in New Mexico had been based largely upon concern for the missionary effort, officials in Mexico City and Madrid agreed to finance the supply caravans as a display of their commitment to the Franciscan enterprise.[6] Although funds from the royal treasury paid for the wagons, supplies, and personnel that comprised the convoys, the missionaries enjoyed direct control over the management and provisioning of the wagons throughout most of the century.[7] But

125

because the caravan offered the only relatively safe means of transport to and from New Mexico, settlers, entrepreneurs, royal officials, and messengers also relied upon the convoy in their travels between New Spain and the northern province.

In theory, the convoy system was to operate on a three-year cycle. Typically, a caravan of about thirty wagons laden with mission supplies—building material, church ornaments, cloth, and nonperishable foodstuffs—left Mexico City in midsummer accompanied by friars and government officials newly appointed to serve in New Mexico, settlers and traders, a complement of a dozen soldiers, and a handful of Indian porters.[8] Their departure was timed so that the worst leg of the trek, from Santa Bárbara to Santa Fe, could be completed during the less forbidding months of late fall and early winter. Arriving in Santa Fe in December or early January, the convoy would spend the next six months unloading and then taking on salt, piñon, hides, and, occasionally, Athapaskan slaves. Timing its journey to avoid crossing the Río del Norte during the spring floods, the convoy left Santa Fe in May or June bound for the markets of Santa Bárbara and its surrounding mining camps. After completing the six-month return to Mexico City, the Franciscan agents in charge of the wagons would spend the next year and a half gathering supplies and outfitting the caravan for its next journey northward.[9]

In actuality, though, service to the northern province could be extremely erratic. Bureaucratic disputes over funding and the administration of the convoy could delay preparations for months. Having missed the window for safe passage that avoided the more treacherous weather of the northern desert, the caravan was then forced to post-

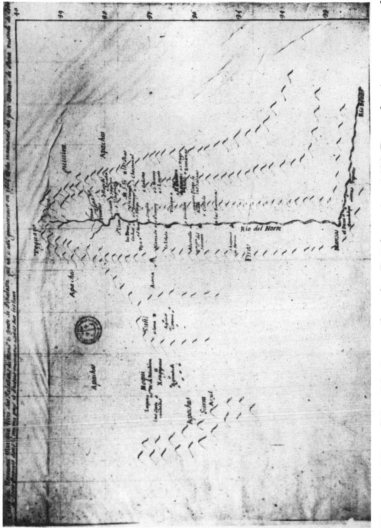

Figure 6. Map of New Mexico attributed to Peñalosa, circa 1680. Reproduction courtesy of the Museum of New Mexico, negative no. 102249.

pone its departure until the following summer, if not longer. Throughout the 1620s, for example, convoys reached Santa Fe only once every four years, arriving in late 1621, 1625, and 1629.[10] In his *Memorial of 1630*, Fray Alonso de Benavides complained that while "it has been stipulated and determined that [the convoy] be done punctually every three years . . . it usually happens that five or six go by without the royal officials' remembering us, and God knows how hard it is for us to ask."[11]

Cognizant of the distance separating them from Mexico City and attuned to the fact that all communication with New Spain depended on the infrequent and sporadic supply caravan, the few Hispanics living in New Mexico grew acutely aware of their isolation from events transpiring in the more cosmopolitan areas of the Spanish colonies. Benavides despaired that "five or six years would pass without our knowing anything of the Spanish nation here in New Mexico."[12]

To remedy the situation, Benavides boldly proposed in his 1630 memorial the opening of an alternate route designed to swing Santa Fe into the mainstream of Spanish colonial society. He calculated a distance of some 250 miles from the plains east of New Mexico to the quasi-mythical bay of Espíritu Santo on the northwestern edge of the Gulf of Mexico. If the crown were to fund a colonization of the plains region and establish a presidio at Espíritu Santo, Benavides reasoned, Santa Fe would have easy access over land to the Gulf coast. From there, a five- or six-day journey by sea would complete a link between New Mexico and the maritime center at Havana. Such a route would cut transportation time to and from the northern province considerably, thereby channeling badly needed traffic in commerce and settlers to the colony.[13]

But because of the inability of seventeenth-century explorers and cartographers to calculate longitudinal distances accurately,[14] Benavides grossly underestimated the distance between Santa Fe and the Gulf coast. Furthermore, his recommendation sparked little interest. As a result, New Mexico remained an isolated and almost forgotten corner of the Spanish realm for the better part of the century.

In addition to its physical isolation, New Mexico was itself a rugged and impoverished territory with little to offer even for those few willing to risk the danger and hardship of the journey up the camino real. The climate was fierce, a difficult transition for newcomers from the more temperate regions of Mexico and Spain. In 1601, one new arrival, Ginés de Herrera Horta, complained of winters lasting up to eight months in the province with cold "so intense that . . . the river freezes over and the Spaniards are always shivering by the fire."[15] He bemoaned the "scarcity of firewood, which has to be brought six or eight leagues to the camps in various carts. The wood is mostly cottonwood from the river valleys and it is so smokey that most of the women and children are in tears night and day."[16] Three decades later, Fray Alonso de Benavides backed up Herrera's claims:

> Suffice it to say that when we are saying Mass we keep a brazier on each side of the chalice; even with this precaution . . . the wine still freezes. Every winter a great number of Indians out in the country are found frozen, and many Spaniards have their ears, feet and hands frozen.[17]

Summers could be equally fierce; they soon earned New Mexico the popular epithet as a "land of 'ocho meses de invierno, cuatro meses de infierno.'"[18]

Reflecting the ruggedness of the province, New Mexico's economy was primitive in comparison with other parts of the empire. Few—if any—of the dreams of wealth that had fueled Oñate's original colonization would find fulfillment during the seventeenth century. The land offered scant resources for exploitation by profit-minded colonists. Although rumors spoke of rich silver veins existing in the mountains west of the Piro pueblos in the early part of the century,[19] no easily exploited deposits of precious metals materialized in the region during the colonial period. What wealth the Hispanic settlers could accumulate rested on the salt and piñon gathered by coerced Pueblo labor, on mantas and hides collected as tribute from the Pueblos or gained in trading fairs with eastern Athapaskans, and on whatever their "industry may bring them in the harvest of wheat and the raising of sheep and goats."[20]

Even those who managed to build sizable stores of such goods faced further obstacles to commercial success. Hard currency was nonexistent in the province during the seventeenth century because of the colonists' failure to uncover precious metals there. To remedy the situation, royal officials in Mexico City briefly considered two methods of artificially inserting coinage into the New Mexican economy. The first involved establishing a mint in the colony and allowing it to stamp coins using an imported metal of lesser importance, such as copper. The second proposed minting coins in New Spain and shipping them north to circulate in the region. The high cost of transportation rendered both proposals unfeasible because, as one official argued, money or bullion sent from New Spain to New Mexico "would circulate at a higher value, and the same would be true of the coin of that land here."[21]

With no circulating currency, trade in New Mexico relied on a system of barter, severely limiting opportunities

130

for capital accumulation from trade on a day-to-day scale. The only hope for exchanging New Mexico's staples for silver or needed goods lay in the markets at Santa Bárbara and, later, El Parral, more than seven hundred miles to the south. But the convoy provided the only reliable means of shipping large quantities of goods to those markets, and space for tradable goods on the southward-bound wagons commanded a premium. Only the church or men of substantial capital and political power—that is, the governor and his favored appointees—could undertake such ventures.[22] Not surprisingly, conflicts between the Franciscans and governors attempting to usurp the right to transport goods on the returning convoy were frequent and explosive.[23]

Difficult access, harsh living conditions, and few opportunities for economic gain offered little to attract immigrants. As a result, only a handful of settlers and traders would find their way up the camino real into New Mexico during the seventeenth century. The Count of Monterrey had foreseen exactly such a fate for the province at the beginning of the century. Writing to King Philip III in 1602, the viceroy observed that New Mexico's settlers

> have nothing to sell from which they can obtain cash, and poverty is everywhere. It therefore seems to me that these conditions, especially the lack of money, will discourage anyone from going there, or, if already settled, would discourage anyone from remaining there. In the Indies no one is content with only food and clothing; it would be difficult, therefore, to take anyone voluntarily from New Spain to New Mexico, especially when both of these things are so limited there, for neither will the food be lavish nor the clothing dignified.[24]

The extant records bear out the viceroy's predictions. In 1677 New Mexico experienced its largest documented influx of newcomers since Oñate's entrada, when forty-three new soldiers entered the province. Of those, forty were convicts sentenced to serve in the desolate northern province and transported there in chains.[25]

Demographic evidence for the seventeenth century is scarce, but the little documentation that survives confirms that few new settlers entered the province over the course of the century. At the time of the decision to maintain the colony in January 1609, almost sixty of the original two hundred fifty or so Spanish settlers remained in New Mexico, thirty of whom were adult males "capable of bearing arms."[26] Later that same year, the arrival of Governor Peralta with sixteen soldiers, six friars, and two lay brothers pushed the number of adult males in the colony over fifty.[27] Eight years later, the Hispanics numbered forty-eight "soldiers and residents."[28]

By 1620 in New Mexico, there was "no other Spanish town except the villa of Santa Fe, which contains fifty residents," and the number of friars in the region stood at sixteen.[29] In his *Revised Memorial of 1634*, Fray Alonso de Benavides estimated the population of Hispanics in Santa Fe to be 250, but this figure is almost certainly exaggerated.[30] In 1639 there were thirty Hispanic families in the land, and "perhaps 200 persons, Spaniards and *mestizos*, able to bear arms."[31] Writing in 1661, Fray Alonso de Posadas lamented that "this land . . . does not have more than a hundred citizens, more or less, and among this number are mulattoes, *mestizos*, and all who have any Spanish blood, even though it is slight."[32]

The demographic record falls silent for the two generations between the time of Posada's remark and the revolt in 1680. A general census of the province was supposedly conducted in 1660, but no record of that undertaking has yet surfaced.[33] A general muster of the refugees fleeing south in September 1680 clarifies the demographic picture somewhat, but historians so far have failed to examine this document closely enough to cast an accurate projection of New Mexico's Hispanic population on the eve of the revolt. Instead, traditional historiography has tended to use the 1680 muster and what is known of the events surrounding its completion to grossly overestimate the nonaboriginal population in the days preceding the rebellion.

As they fled down the Río del Norte in the summer of 1680, Otermín and Lieutenant Governor García guessed the number of refugees in their respective parties to be 1,000 and 1,500, respectively. A precise count of those refugees, taken when the parties had combined and reached La Salineta in late September 1680, revealed that 1,946 persons had escaped the northern province, with the added mention that a handful of settlers evaded the muster by deserting camp and entering Nueva Vizcaya in spite of Otermín's orders to the contrary. By factoring the report of 401 persons dead or missing in the uprising—a figure generated by Otermín in the turmoil of the first days of the revolt—into their overall calculations, historians have tended to arrive at a figure of between 2,500 and 3,000 for the number of Hispanic settlers residing in New Mexico just prior to the outbreak of violence.[34]

A more careful tabulation of the data reveals that such an estimate is markedly inflated. Of the 1,946 persons counted by Otermín at La Salineta, 837 were listed specifically as Indian servants, refugees from the Piro pueblos, or "Mexican Indians," along with their dependents residing in New Mexico. Non-Europeans also made up an unknowable portion of another 281 persons lumped into a general category as the undefined dependents and servants of those signing the muster list. And although a majority of the 211 adult males counted as Hispanics were recorded as married, the record offers no information on the ethnic background of their spouses (nor, for that matter, the women's names). Considering the widespread incidence of miscegenation in the colony throughout the seventeenth century,[35] it is not unreasonable to assume that a significant proportion of these women were of Amerindian, not European, background.

Finally, it is likely that Otermín's figure of 401 settlers killed in the Pueblo uprising was incorrect. In the La Salineta muster, only 53 persons listed specifically as members of Hispanic families were declared dead or missing, along with 95 casualties made up of an unspecified mix of Hispanic dependents and Indian servants. Although these figures include neither Hispanics who were killed but left no relatives to declare their loss nor the 21 friars martyred in the rebellion, it is likely that more Hispanics survived to partake in the La Salineta muster than either Otermín or later historians calculated.[36]

With this tabulation in mind, a more reasonable estimate of the number of people of European background residing in New Mexico on the eve of the revolt stands near one thousand—and clearly the Hispanic population numbered only in the hundreds for the majority of the pre-revolt period. Moreover, it would seem that the steady, if unspectacular, rise in that population in the generations before 1680 stemmed more from internal growth than from any meaningful influx of settlers from the south. In 1680, Otermín alluded to the fact that New Mexico had received little in the way of new colonists during the seventeenth century when he noted that "in the case of everyone in this kingdom [of New Mexico], if one avoids a son or a brother he lights upon a nephew or a cousin, and when one is touched they all cry out."[37] The El Paso muster rolls of 1681 supported the governor's contention. Of the 147 men counted, 131 were New Mexico natives, while only sixteen were natives of Mexico and Spain.[38]

Thus, as the century progressed, the majority of "Spanish" settlers in New Mexico were born, lived, and died in the northern province, never having seen Mexico, much less Spain, except through occasional tales spun by newly arrived friars, governors, or infrequent wanderers who found their way to this remote corner of the empire. The world for these first few generations of colonists was a New Mexico of arid deserts, rugged mountains, and desolate highland plains. Most importantly, it was a world inhabited in overwhelming numbers by its native peoples, the Pueblo Indians. Over four generations, New Mexico's aboriginal inhabitants would exert a profound influence on the tiny Hispanic community, compounding the colony's isolation by driving a cultural and, especially, a biological wedge between the members of the northern colony and their European counterparts in the mainstream of Spanish colonial society to the south.

Chapter Seven

Acculturation and Miscegenation

The Changing Face of the Spanish Presence in New Mexico

New Mexico and its native inhabitants together exerted a profound influence upon the handful of Hispanics who called the territory home in the seventeenth century. The land made life hard on those unable to withstand its furies, breaking some and bending others to a shape and appearance as rugged as the terrain itself. Pueblo culture, with a tradition and a social order dating back centuries, resisted Spanish efforts toward a guided change of its values, beliefs, and ideals. Immersed in this culture, Hispanic colonists could not escape adopting many of its aspects. Pueblo ways, so foreign and so savage to the original colonists in the closing years of the sixteenth century, became second nature to subsequent generations of settlers. Over the course of the seventeenth century, the forces of nature and acculturation combined to bury Oñate's vi-

sion of Spanish domination through cultural separation and superiority. In time, the faces of the Hispanic settlers changed so markedly that they would have been unrecognizable to their predecessors in the ranks of Oñate's followers.

In 1598, Captain Luis Gasco de Velasco had presented himself for the conquest of New Mexico, a man twenty-eight years old, crimson bearded and of medium stature, and a native of Cuenca, Spain.[1] An inventory of his possessions to be taken on the expedition northward revealed personal effects of a decidedly European sort:

First, he exhibited and brought before his lordship a standard of figured white Castilian silk, with fringes and trimmings of gold and crimson silk. . . .

Item: A silver lance, in its handle, for the exercise of his office as captain, with tassels of gold and yellow and purple silk.

Item: Three sets of horse armor of buckskin, lined with undressed leather, for the flanks, foreheads, breasts, necks—all, without anything lacking.

Item: A sword and a gilded dagger with their waist belts stitched with purple, yellow, and white silk.

Item: One bed with two mattresses, a coverlet, sheets, pillow-cases, pillows, and a canvas mattress-bag bound with leather. . . .

Item: One suit of blue Italian velvet trimmed with wide gold pasementerie, consisting of doublet, breeches, and green silk stockings with blue garters with points of gold lace. . . .

Item: Another suit of Chinese flowered silk. . . .

Item: Eight pairs of Cordovan leather boots, six white pairs, and four black, and four pairs of laced gaiters.

137

Item: Two hats, one black, trimmed around the crown with a silver cord, with black, purple, and white feathers and the other gray, with yellow and purple feathers.[2]

The complete list filled three pages of text.

Sixty-five years later, an immense cultural and genetic gap had emerged to separate Velasco from his counterpart in a drastically changed New Mexican Hispanic society of the 1660s. Nicolás de Aguilar, at various times holder of the offices of field captain, sergeant, and adjutant in the villa of Santa Fe and alcalde mayor of the district Las Salinas, stood before the tribunal of the Inquisition in Mexico City on April 12, 1663. His examiners described him as a thirty-six-year-old man "of large body, coarse and somewhat brown," a mestizo, a reputed murderer, and an accused heretic.[3] Dressed in flannel trousers and woolen shirt and stockings—all crudely woven and in places badly frayed—and wearing a cotton neckcloth and buckskin shoes of the type commonly worn by colonists in New Mexico, Aguilar handed his inquisitors the key to a small wooden box that had accompanied him on his journey from the northern province. The box contained all of the accused's possessions, collected in New Mexico and sent south by commissary Posadas for closer scrutiny by his superiors in the Holy Office in the viceregal capital. Upon opening it, Aguilar's examiners found only a collection of well-worn clothing and a few personal items that included

3. A doublet of buff and black wool, badly worn, with cotton sleeves embroidered with blue wool. . . .
5. Item. An old cotton shirt, adorned with drawn work.
6. Item. Another cloth shirt, worn out. . . .
12. One pair of shoes of Córdovan leather, worn out.
13. A book, entitled, "Catechism in the Castilian and

Timuquana languages." Inside of this was another very small book, entitled, "Instructions for examining the conscience."

14. A bar of soap and a little *alucema* wrapped in an old black rag.

15. An antelope skin muffler lined with yellow linen.

16. A cloth containing, apparently, roots of dry grass, which he said they call bear grass in New Mexico, used for curing fevers.

17. Three small pieces of dried grass roots, which he said is called *manso* grass, and is good for healing wounds. . . .

21. A rosary strung on *coyole* wire, having large beads, and a little silver cross. . . .

25. A buckskin bag within which is a cotton pillow filled with sheep's wool.

26. A mattress of coarse black and white stuff, filled with sheep's wool.[4]

As a mestizo, Aguilar represented what had become, by the time of his birth in the third decade of the seventeenth century, a large proportion of the Hispanic population in the province. Isolated among an overwhelming native population, Hispanics in New Mexico inevitably intermixed with Pueblo Indians. Even before the mass desertion of the colony in 1601, only forty-two of the region's two hundred male Spaniards had brought families with them from the south.[5] No quantitative data exist, but surviving documentary evidence indicates that Pueblo and Spanish ancestries blended at a rate sufficient to alarm those conservative members of the colony who were convinced of the need to maintain clear lines of European heritage in the midst of a Pueblo majority.

Pointing to the results of more than a generation of miscegenation within the province, Fray Esteban de Perea, commissary of the Holy Office in New Mexico at that time, lamented in 1631 that in presiding over the duties of the Inquisition he was forced to deal with a population that contained "so many *mestizos, mulattos,* and bastards, and others [who are] worse . . . and of [such] little moral strength that I am sometimes confused [by their testimonies in these investigations]."[6] Three decades later, Inquisition officials attempted to deflate Governor Peñalosa's air of self-importance during the latter's appearance before the tribunal by reminding him that "he was merely the governor and captain general of fifty men, [composed] of the dregs of the earth, *mestizos* and mulattoes."[7]

Further evidence of widespread miscegenation in the colony lies in the fact that as the century progressed many mestizos and others of mixed racial background attained official positions in New Mexico's colonial government, a rare phenomenon in other parts of a rigidly caste-oriented Spanish-American empire.[8] No development reflects more accurately the scarcity of Spanish "pure-bloods" to fill vital posts in New Mexico. During Rosas's administration, one friar objected to the governor's manipulation of the elections for the 1639–41 cabildo and referred to the men who eventually won seats on the council as "those four *mestizo* dogs."[9] Decades later, the ranks of officials of mixed heritage included not only Nicolás de Aguilar but also Captain Francisco de Ortega, listed in 1669 as a mulatto;[10] Juan Luján, in 1665 the alcalde mayor of Los Taos and a *mestizo amulatado;*[11] Joseph Nieto, in 1667 the mulatto alcalde mayor of Las Salinas;[12] and Alonso García, lieutenant governor of New Mexico in 1680, head official of Spanish colonial authority for the entire Río Abajo region, and a mestizo.[13]

The destabilizing effect of such a large mestizo population among the colonials in New Mexico cannot be over-emphasized. Looked down upon by Hispanics of pure blood as "half-breeds" and yet in many cases expected to fill roles of responsibility in the colony, mestizos found themselves pushed in different directions by the deep-seated ambivalence prevalent among the Spanish settlers. Such social pressures could prove explosive and gave rise to frequent incidents of violence and confrontation. In 1639, Diego Martín, a mestizo, led an uprising in the pueblo of Taos that resulted in the deaths of the Franciscan friar in residence and two soldiers.[14] During Governor López de Mendizábal's administration (1659–62) and his legalization of the kachinas, many friars feared the role that mestizos might take in the turmoil generated by the Pueblo cultural revival. Fray Alonso de Posadas expressed concern over the effect that such an atmosphere would have, "especially [on] those of low degree, such as *mestizos*."[15]

Nicolás de Aguilar only confirmed the Franciscan's fears. Upon his excommunication by custodian García de San Francisco in 1660, the mestizo simply rose "from the place where he was, putting on his hat and turning his back, [and] replied to the judge that he did not care for all the excommunications in the world."[16] Frustrated, San Francisco resigned his duties as ecclesiastical judge, "saying that he did not wish to proceed with people who had no fear of God or of censures."[17] Emblematic of a Hispanic society that had forsaken its distance from the surrounding Pueblo populace, New Mexico's mestizo presence could not be ignored.

At the same time, many mestizos capitalized on their poorly defined status in seventeenth-century New Mexico, moving extensively—if often clandestinely—within both Pueblo and Hispanic social circles.[18] In doing so, these

141

"crossovers" served as important intermediaries in a process of acculturation that over the course of the century slowly blurred the lines differentiating European newcomer from Pueblo Indian. But mestizos were only one of many vectors by which Pueblo culture penetrated the Hispanic community. The colonists' isolation from events transpiring to the south and their numerically small presence in a land where the indigenous inhabitants numbered in the tens of thousands meant that everyday contacts between Hispanic settlers and Pueblo Indians were as extensive as they were inevitable. Openings for settlers to learn of and accept Pueblo ways proved ubiquitous. As time wore on and as the newcomers seized these opportunities to gain from Pueblo convention and experience, important changes transpired in the life-style of New Mexico's colonists.

Hispanic exposure to the Pueblos—their style of living, their attitudes and beliefs, their folk practices—began in childhood. In the schools of religious instruction run by the friars, Hispanic and Pueblo boys learned together, sang together, and, presumably, played together, in many ways closing the gap that separated their parents' worlds.[19] Apparently this process began almost as soon as Oñate's original colonists entered the region. As early as 1601, Ginés de Herrera Horta told of meeting in New Mexico "a Spanish boy, who, as the lad himself told him, grew up among the Indian boys. He knew the language of the Picurís or Queres better than the Indians themselves, and they were astonished to hear him talk."[20] Several decades later, this first generation of New Mexico–raised Hispanics reached adulthood and assumed roles of leadership within the colony, causing Fray Esteban de Perea to complain in 1628 of conditions "in this new land and among this people, raised from childhood with the customs of these Indians, with neither decency nor schools . . . who blossom out as captains and royal officials."[21]

Certainly one of the major factors that pushed Hispanic settlers into accepting Pueblo practices was the extremely limited availability of medical care in the European sense of the term. No institutionally trained and licensed physicians or surgeons practiced in the northern province during the seventeenth century. Instead, the filling of this niche fell to those members of the colony who generally boasted the highest level of formal education—the Franciscan missionaries. Very little has survived to illuminate the manner in which the friars carried out this charge in the missions and throughout the Hispanic community, but it is evident that the church did attach importance to caring for its followers during times of sickness. By 1631 the Franciscans had established an infirmary for the colony that, documentary evidence suggests, was located in the mission at San Felipe.[22] The arrival of the triennial caravan brought with it supplies for that infirmary: linens, medicinal herbs and preserves, and a few basic surgical instruments.[23] In addition, each pair of friars serving in the missionary field received a copper cupping instrument, one syringe, a razor, one lancet, and a pair of barber scissors, indicating that bloodletting and other minor invasive procedures were practiced with some frequency in the missions.[24]

Still, it is doubtful whether care at the hands of the friars was a practical or even an attractive option for the majority of those Hispanics stricken with illness in New Mexico during the seventeenth century. Thirty miles separated the most important European settlement at Santa Fe from the infirmary at San Felipe, making access to that facility impractical for most colonists. Throughout the province, the small number of friars and their wide geographic dispersion meant long traveling distances for those needing medical attention but not living in the shadow of a mission with a friar in residence. Logistical problems aside, it is not hard to imagine the reluctance with which many settlers viewed the prospect of submitting to therapy at the end of a razor wielded by a priest with little or no formal medical training.

These factors combined with the constant interaction between Hispanic settlers and the surrounding Pueblo majority to make indigenous folk medicine and *curanderismo* the preferred options for relief from illness, facilitating the process by which Pueblo ways gained acceptance and permeated the European community. In addition to documenting Aguilar's possession of bear grass (used, apparently, for curing fevers) and manso grass for healing wounds, Inquisition testimonies from this period reveal many examples of Hispanic settlers in New Mexico turning to Pueblo Indians in search of medicines, aphrodisiacs, and love potions.

Franciscans in seventeenth-century New Mexico recognized as well as any cultural anthropologist or ethnohistorian working among twentieth-century Pueblo communities that native medicinal practices intertwined tightly with Pueblo cosmology and worldviews. Dismayed references to Hispanic settlers' having resorted to Pueblo cure-alls appear with impressive frequency in the Inquisition documents from the period. Charges of nativism and "sorcery" leveled against a colonist often spurred the commissary of the Holy Office to embark on lengthy inquiries into the accused's private affairs. Something of the flavor of daily life in New Mexico's Hispanic commu-

Figure 7. "Eagle Dancer—San Ildefonso" (E. S. Curtis, 1925). Photograph courtesy of the Smithsonian Institution Libraries, negative no. 94-1510.

nity has been preserved in the testimonies generated by these investigations. At the same time, the documents provide an invaluable glimpse into the manner in which members of the European population opened themselves to an acceptance of Pueblo ways.

One illustrative example of this cultural transmission from Pueblo to Hispanic society is that of Beatriz de los Angeles. A mestiza and the widow of alférez Juan de la Cruz, de los Angeles lived on an estancia amid the Tano pueblos southwest of Santa Fe. Throughout the 1620s, she enjoyed a reputation among the Hispanic community as a "sorceress of compassion" or, more clearly, a *curandera* who proffered home remedies and incantations from the vantage point of one who moved in both Indian and European circles.[25] Supporters recounted the tale of how de los Angeles traveled to Senecú in 1628 to help doña María Granillo overcome a serious illness. There, while in the company of "other witches," the curandera apparently saved her patient's life by playing patoles with Granillo and simultaneously reciting a number of spells.[26]

But de los Angeles's reputed talents included more than the ability to cure illness through shamanism. For years, women in the Hispanic community had sought her help in curbing the amorous pursuits of wayward husbands. Usually, de los Angeles answered these requests by prescribing *gusanos ciegos*, a type of worm gathered easily in any dung heap in the region, and directing her clients to hide them in the food eaten by the men in question.[27] Problems arose for de los Angeles, however, at the close of the decade when she gave this concoction to her own partner, Diego Bellido. Bellido grew violently ill upon ingesting a bowl of milk laced with the worms, and when de los Angeles attempted to nullify the potion by giving Bellido an unspecified oil as an emetic, his condition only worsened, leading ultimately to his death.[28] The incident drew the attention of commissary Estevan de Perea and generated a lengthy investigation by the Inquisition into de los Angeles's activities.

Numerous examples also survive of colonial settlers approaching Pueblo Indians directly in search of folk remedies. To the dismay of inquisitors like Perea, these requests exposed Hispanics to Pueblo practices steeped in native ceremony and religious tradition. On March 25, 1631, Ana Cadimo testified that at some time in 1629 she had approached a Tewa woman from San Ildefonso named Francisca Latiphaña in the hope of acquiring relief from a chronic ailment. Known for her experience in dealing with peyote, Latiphaña provided Cadimo with a cup containing a mixture of herbs dissolved in water. Before allowing Cadimo to drink the liquid, the curandera performed some unspecified chants and incantations. After drinking the concoction, Cadimo saw visions in the cup and imagined hearing music and what she thought were voices.

Although she did not comment on the efficacy of the therapy, it is interesting to note that in the same testimony Cadimo admitted to having approached a number of Pueblos a year later, again claiming to be in need of relief. She was told that she had been bewitched from quarters unknown and was given instructions to find an old Keres Indian from San Marcos. This medicine man, her native sources claimed, would provide her with enough peyote to cure her ills and enable her to visualize the person who had bewitched her. Cadimo followed the instructions but again declined to comment on their effectiveness during Perea's interrogation. As a postscript, Cadimo noted that at the time of her testimony the curandera who originally gave her peyote in 1629 continued to sell the drug to people of

147

Santa Fe, promoting it now as a means of seeing great distances and identifying persons as they approached New Mexico along the camino real.[29]

More often, however, Hispanic settlers turned in their search for potions and cure-alls to the most convenient source of Pueblo knowledge—native relatives, household servants, and casual acquaintances. In June 1631, Juana de los Reyes testified that in order to halt her husband's extramarital affair she had approached a Keres woman serving in the household of Captain Diego de Santa Cruz for advice. The woman's recommendation was simple: "Take the urine of your husband's mistress and mix it with dog manure," she told de los Reyes, "and with that your husband and the woman will come to hate one another and he will continue to love you."[30] In a similar predicament in 1629, María Márquez sought the council of Alonso Gutiérrez's sister-in-law, a Tewa named Isabel Quagua. This time the instructions called for Márquez to take her husband's urine, mix it with unspecified herbs, and smear the potion on the doorstep of the man's new lover. This, the Tewa claimed, would sour the illicit romance.[31] Both women admitted to carrying out the instructions, but apparently neither remedy accomplished the desired effect.

Similarly, on November 4, 1661, María de Abisu testified that twenty-four years earlier, while in the company of her sister-in-law, doña María de Abedaño, the two women encountered an acquaintance of Abedaño's, an Indian from San Cristóbal named Pablo. Troubled by an unrequited love,

> the aforesaid Doña María de Abedaño asked [Abisu], as a person who understood the language of the Indian, to tell him to give her some herbs which would cause a man to love her very much and never forget her. The deponent

148

went away to the garden, leaving the Indian and the aforesaid Doña María de Abedaño alone together; but she does not know what they said. . . . She does know that the Indian gave her the herbs . . . and that the woman is now married to the same man.[32]

Hispanic exposures to indigenous customs in New Mexico were not limited to the Pueblos, though; settlers also accepted and actively participated in ceremonial rites performed by the region's Athapaskan nomads. One documented example survives from 1660. In August of that year, Governor López de Mendizábal sent Diego Romero, alcalde ordinario of the villa of Santa Fe, and five other men to trade for buffalo hides and antelope skins among the Jicarilla Apaches on the Great Plains. Upon reaching the encampment of one Apache group, Romero exchanged pleasantries with the Indians and "asked them if they did not remember his father . . . [giving] them to understand by signs that he was a ruddy man who had come at such and such a time . . . and that he had left a son with an Indian woman among those Heathen, and that he himself was going to leave another." A long discussion among the Apaches ensued, which culminated in a ceremony later described by an eyewitness:

> At about four in the afternoon they brought a tent of new leather and set it up in the field; they then brought two bundles, one of antelope skins, and the other of buffalo skins, which they placed near the tent. Then they brought another large new buffalo skin which they stretched on the ground and put Diego Romero upon it, lying on his back. They then began to dance the *catzina*, making turns, singing, and raising up and laying Diego Romero down again on the skin in accordance with the movement of the dance of the catzina. When the dance was ended about nightfall, they put him again on the skin,

and taking it by the corners, drew him into the tent, into which they brought him a maiden, whom they left with him the entire night. On the next day in the morning the captains of the rancherias came to see whether Diego Romero had known the woman carnally; seeing that he had known her, they anointed Diego Romero's breast with the blood. They then put a feather on his head, in his hair, and proclaimed him as their captain.[33]

Countless numbers of similar testimonies fill the Inquisition documents from this period in New Mexico's history. Together, they paint a picture of the day-to-day lives of Hispanics in the northern colony, evoking images of an uneventful and rustic existence broken only by rumors and excited gossip about illicit affairs, failed romances, and perceived lapses into nativism and superstitious practices among neighbors, friends, or relatives. Perea himself, in carrying out his charge as commissary of the Holy Office, lamented what he judged to be the backwardness of the colony and decried the frequency with which its non-aboriginal inhabitants, "simple people [who] had no proper fear of [native] powders [and] herbs," displayed only a minimal comprehension of the teachings of the Catholic church.[34]

More importantly, however, these testimonies freeze for the historical record a dynamic that slowly eroded the cultural barrier separating Pueblo and European worlds. This process of acculturation would prove crucial to undercutting Spanish political authority in the region over the course of the seventeenth century. By 1680, New Mexico had become a backwash relative to the mainstream of Spanish-American colonial society, as Pueblos and Athapaskans wrought deep ethnic and cultural changes on the small European community over four generations. All

vestiges of Oñate's dialectic of domination through physical distance and cultural segregation had vanished. Now a
person of familiarity and even intimacy with the Pueblos,
the Hispanic's position of authority stood in jeopardy.

Chapter Eight

A Colony Lost

The nineteen years from the close of
Mendizábal's tenure as governor of New
Mexico until 1680 were difficult ones for
the region's Hispanics as they struggled
to maintain a precarious hold over the
province. External threats in the form of
natural disasters and ever-more-fre-
quent depredations by Athapaskans
called European authority into question
for a steadily growing number of Pueblos. At the same time, the strains of more
than three generations of Franciscan and
Spanish colonial rule began to wear
heavily on the Pueblos, inflicting suffering to an unprecedented degree upon
New Mexico's native inhabitants.

As the European presence grew increasingly intolerable, many Pueblos'
thoughts focused less on simple accommodation and the clandestine preserving
of traditional ways and looked instead to
direct confrontation as the best means by

which to free themselves from the hardships of colonial rule. This growing dissatisfaction among the Pueblos now combined with continuing subversion of the "Spanish" presence in the region to decisively challenge Hispanic control over the land and its people.

Of the transformations and hardships inflicted upon Pueblo society in the seventeenth century, none was more devastating than the steady decline in native population. Yet no facet of Spanish-Pueblo contact is more poorly understood by twentieth-century scholars, a fact due mainly to the paucity of demographic evidence for Pueblo communities in the pre-revolt period. Although a general census compiled for the province in 1660 was reported by Vetancurt in the eighteenth century, no copy of that effort has surfaced in the historical record.[1] Similarly lost are the seventeenth-century mission baptismal and burial records so crucial to understanding the effects of epidemic diseases among the Pueblos, probably because of the destruction of doctrinal archives during the revolt itself.[2]

But enough evidence survives in the form of estimates of native population by contemporary chroniclers to suggest that the Pueblos suffered an uninterrupted decline in numbers over a period encompassing more than two centuries. Population losses among the region's native peoples began early in the sixteenth century, possibly pre-dating even the first direct Pueblo-European contact in 1539. Because sixteenth-century Pueblo society formed one part of a network of trade and communication that spanned much of the North American continent,[3] it is unlikely that the Pueblos escaped the pandemics of European disease that swept the New World shortly after the first Spanish landfalls in Central America and Mexico. Quickly outstripping the advances made by their European carriers, Old

World diseases such as smallpox, influenza, and measles often visited death upon remote indigenous communities long before the arrival of any Spaniard among them.[4] From 1519 to 1524, for instance, smallpox—reportedly introduced by a member of the Pánfilo de Narváez expedition on the Veracruz coast—spread at least as far south as Chile and across most of North America. Contemporary estimates placed the mortality resulting from this first American smallpox epidemic as high as 50 percent for some Amerindian communities, and there can be little doubt that those left dead in the illness's wake numbered in the millions.[5]

The historical and archaeological record is all too silent for this chapter of Pueblo history, but there is little chance that New Mexico's native inhabitants escaped the European-introduced epidemic diseases that devastated Amerindian societies throughout the New World. Alvar Núñez Cabeza de Vaca and his companions are known to have unleashed some type of contagious illness among native groups as they passed nearby in the early 1530s.[6] By the time Oñate and his colonists arrived in 1598, population decline among the Pueblos was already well advanced. Estimates place the number of inhabited pueblos at the time of European contact in 1539 at between 110 and 150.[7] In 1581, nine members of the Chamuscado-Rodríguez expedition counted 61 pueblos in their travels through the area and agreed on a total population for those towns of 130,000 persons.[8] Although it is impossible to verify the accuracy of this figure, when it is compared with Oñate's estimate of 60,000 two decades later,[9] it becomes apparent that New Mexico had begun to lose vast numbers of its aboriginal inhabitants long before the establishment of the first permanent European colony. Losses would continue over subsequent generations, with New Mexico's Pueblo population reaching a nadir in the early eighteenth century. In 1706, the Pueblos, excluding the Hopi groups, numbered 6,440 Indians spread among 18 pueblos.[10]

Although northern New Mexico's demographic crisis extended over more than two centuries, the decline during the eight decades between Oñate's entrada and the revolt of 1680 weighed most heavily upon Pueblo society. All evidence indicates that Pueblo losses continued unabated throughout this period. In 1638, Fray Juan de Prada reckoned the number of Pueblos in the province to be 40,000 "or a little less,"[11] a significant decrease from Oñate's turn-of-the-century estimate of 60,000. Four decades later, Fray Francisco de Ayeta counted 17,000 Pueblos in the region in what by then numbered only 46 pueblos.[12] Two factors stand out in the documentary record as the primary causes of the decline: continued Pueblo suffering from European diseases, and sporadic episodes of drought that combined with the harsh demands of the Spanish colonial system to generate devastating famines and hardship for the region's native inhabitants.

Documentary evidence for episodes of epidemic disease in New Mexico during this period is scarce, but a few scattered references suggest that outbreaks occurred with sufficient frequency and ferocity to fuel the major portion of the Pueblo population decline. In making his estimate of 40,000 Pueblos in 1638, Juan de Prada pointed out with alarm that his count indicated a loss of more than one-third of the Indian population since the early years of the colony. The Franciscan had no doubts as to the cause of the decline: the number of Pueblos had "diminished to that extent on account of the very active prevalence during these last years of smallpox and the sickness that the

155

Mexicans called *cocolitzli*."[13] Two years later, widespread illness descended again upon the northern province, this time claiming more than 3,000 Pueblo victims.[14] And in 1671, Fray Francisco de Ayeta lamented the appearance of "a great pestilence, which . . . carried off many people and cattle."[15]

Interspersed between these outbreaks—and at times closely associated with them—came famine. Before the arrival of the Spaniards, Pueblo survival in a region plagued by unpredictable weather and frequent periods of sterility had depended on a complex system of barter in which one community's surplus made up for another's shortfall.[16] In the seventeenth century, however, European demands shattered this fragile balance of survival. Old trade networks dried up quickly as Franciscan control over Pueblo land and livestock ensured that surplus goods remained locked in mission storehouses. Pueblo subsistence now depended entirely upon the friars during times of hardship, a potent weapon of coercion wielded by Franciscans bent on maintaining native compliance with the demands of mission life. This fact did not escape the attention of New Mexico's Hispanic inhabitants, several of whom testified in 1663 that during a recent period of famine, "the convents of Senecú, Socorro, La Isleta, Taxique, Cuarac, and others, which had some wheat, corn, and cattle, when these were sought for, gave on every Sunday during all the time of famine an entire week's ration to their parishioners to keep them from wandering away."[17]

Tribute demands by colonial officials and encomenderos only aggravated Pueblo suffering and dependence upon their European overlords, a burden that became increasingly acute as the century progressed. Dismayed at the steady decline of the native populace and anxious to maintain even the modest income they enjoyed in the form of Pueblo payments, settlers and government officials refused to adjust tribute requirements downward to compensate for the dwindling number of tributaries. Instead, in an effort to reverse the fall in revenue, the crown's representatives raised tribute levels in 1643 and in the process increased exponentially the burden of taxation that fell on surviving Pueblos. Henceforth, tribute consisted of one manta and one *fanega* of corn paid quarterly. More importantly, this payment was now collected from each individual of tributary age, not from each household as in previous years.[18]

As the number of Pueblos continued to fall and tributary burdens steadily worsened, the Pueblos fell increasingly vulnerable to the devastating effects of drought and famine. With neither personal nor communal reserves of food to sustain them, a stricken pueblo's inhabitants survived only at the mercy of the nearest Franciscan missionary, and failing that, perhaps not at all. In 1666, for example, widespread drought struck the province of New Mexico. With no crops to harvest for the next four years, Pueblo and Hispanic alike suffered tremendously. But the greatest hardship fell upon the native populace, since the Europeans expropriated the land's few remaining staples. By 1669, the situation was desperate. On April 1, Fray Juan Bernal wrote to Mexico City:

> For three years now no crops have been harvested. In the past year, 1668, a great many Indians perished of hunger, lying dead along the roads, in the ravines, and in their huts. There were pueblos (as instance Humanos) where more than 450 died of hunger. The same calamity still prevails, for, because of lack of money, there is not a *fanega* of corn or of wheat in the whole kingdom, so that

Figure 8. "San Juan Woman Gathering Chilies" (E. S. Curtis, 1905). Photograph courtesy of the National Anthropological Archives, Smithsonian Institution, negative no. 79-4761.

for two years the food of the Spaniards, men and women alike, had been the hides of cattle which they had in their houses. . . . And the greatest misfortune of all is that they can no longer find a bit of leather to eat, for their herds are dying.[19]

The suffering continued through 1670, with much of the populace still subsisting on leather straps and hides, "preparing them for food by soaking and washing them and toasting them in the fire with maize, and boiling them with herbs. By this means almost half the people in the province escaped" starvation.[20] A new round of epidemic disease arriving in 1671 only added to the province's woes, carving off its own share of victims.[21]

These hardships devastated Pueblo society and provided ample opportunity for native leaders—already chafing to rid the land of its European newcomers—to point out the harm that would inevitably accompany a continued colonial presence. With their people starving and their children perishing in wave after wave of previously unknown but now hauntingly familiar diseases, many Pueblos found less and less solace in the preaching and relief efforts of the missionaries and yearned for a means to regain control over their own survival. At the same time, the most practical reason for enduring life under the colonial yoke—military protection by the Hispanic settlers—all but disappeared as those forces proved increasingly impotent in the face of renewed hostilities by surrounding Apaches.

Colonial authorities had done little to alleviate the Apache threat in the years since the first outbreaks of violence in 1606–1607. On the contrary, over the course of the century many of New Mexico's governors had aggravated tensions between Pueblo, Apache, and Hispanic in their efforts to accumulate wealth in the northern province. Several holders of the office went so far as to instigate hostilities with the nomads, since military campaigns against the region's Athapaskan groups offered a pretext for taking prisoners who could either be used as slaves or sold as such for a considerable profit. Fray García de San Francisco described this practice succinctly in a letter to the viceroy in the early stages of López de Mendizábal's administration:

> Very great, Sir, has been the covetousness of the governors of this kingdom, wherein they have, under color of chastising the neighboring enemy, made opportunity to send, apparently in the service of his Majesty, squadrons of men to capture the heathen Indians to send them to camp and the mines of El Parral to sell (as governor Don Bernardo López de Mendizábal is doing at present, he having sent there more than seventy Indian men and women to be sold.) This is a thing which his Majesty and the señores viceroys have forbidden, under penalty of disgrace, deprivation of office, and loss of property, but no attention is paid to the order on account of the great interests involved; hence God, our Lord, through this inhuman practice is losing innumerable souls of the heathen hereabout, who have from fear of it, conceived a mortal hatred for our holy faith and enmity for the Spanish nation.[22]

That enmity took the form of violent reprisals by provoked Apache bands. Sometimes retribution preceded the governor's return to the colony and took aim against the pueblos he had left undefended. San Francisco recounted just such a chain of events, telling how

> for this purpose of making captives, the governor on the fourth of September of this year, 1659, sent out an army of eight hundred Christian Indians and forty Spaniards, though there was evident risk at the time the army set out that trouble would ensue, for the kingdom was then full

of bands of heathen who have entered the pueblos of Las Salinas, the *camino real*, and the farms of El Río, and also into the pueblos of Hemes [Jemez], San Ildefonso, and San Felipe. In these pueblos they have killed some Christian Indians and have carried off others alive to perish in cruel martyrdom. They have also driven off some herds of horses and mares.[23]

Moreover, the Franciscan argued, the diversion of Pueblo labor to these slave-hunting campaigns jeopardized the precious harvests in the region. He noted that

there cannot fail on this account . . . to come great hunger and loss of life, for the army went away at the time when the corn was maturing, and there are eight hundred and forty corn fields left to go ruin without their owners, at the mercy of the bears and other wild beasts, which constantly destroy the crops while the heathen lay waste to one and catch the other.[24]

But the most serious outbreaks of violence generally stemmed from Athapaskan suffering during times of famine. The European disruption of trade and subsistence patterns in New Mexico impinged upon the nomads' ability to weather hard times as dramatically as it did among the Pueblos, forcing them to adopt new strategies or modify old ones in their struggle for survival. Mission storehouses of grain and foodstuffs offered tempting and convenient targets to hungry raiding parties, particularly those who enjoyed the enhanced striking and carrying capacities afforded by the adoption of horses into seventeenth-century Athapaskan society.[25] During the difficult year of 1640, for example, Apache raiders plundered a total of more than 20,000 fanegas (52,000 bushels) of corn throughout the province.[26]

Similarly, the severe drought and famine of 1666–70 brought starving bands of Athapaskans in from the plains

161

in droves, touching off half a decade of unprecedented violence in New Mexico from which European authority would never fully recover. By April 1, 1669, Fray Juan Bernal could write that

> the whole land is at war with the widespread heathen nation of the Apache Indians, who kill all the Christian Indians they can find and encounter. No road is safe; everyone travels at risk of his life, for the heathen traverse them all, being courageous and brave, and they hurl themselves at danger like people who know no God nor that there is any hell.[27]

The province proved poorly equipped for resistance. Famine had greatly thinned the ranks of Christian Indians who could be rallied for defense, and the Hispanic community in 1670 could muster only 170 soldiers from among its own ranks to meet the threat to the colony.[28] Moreover, the disposition of those scant forces left the province easy prey to the nomads' guerilla-style tactics. According to Bernal, even "when the governor has occasion to pursue the enemy after they have committed some sudden outrage, he can scarcely gather twenty men, for most of them live on the frontiers and on farms. Because of such delay the enemy is usually able to escape in safety."[29] Powerless to halt the violence, New Mexico's Hispanics could offer little assistance to native communities such as the Zuñi pueblo of Hawikuh. In 1673 Apache assailants attacked and burned the town, killing two hundred of its inhabitants and the resident friar and carrying away more than a thousand residents and their livestock.[30]

But the raids took their greatest toll among the southeastern pueblos—Senecú and the six of Las Salinas. Apaches spread terror throughout this region during the early 1670s, and the list of Franciscan martyrs grew ever longer as a result. At Senecú, Apaches killed Fray Alonso Gil de Avila in his own *convento*, with five arrows to the chest.[31] At Abó, they sacked and burned the convento after slaying Fray Pedro de Ayala, "stripping him of his clothing, putting a rope around his neck, flogging him most cruelly, and finally killing him with blows of the *macana*; after he was dead they surrounded the body with dead white lambs, and covered the privy parts, leaving him in this way."[32]

Unable to count on Hispanic military protection in the face of such rampant bloodshed, the Tompiro inhabitants of the Salinas pueblos chose to flee, abandoning Humanos, Abó, Chililí, and Tajique in 1672, and Tabira and Quarai at some point shortly thereafter.[33] Some of these Tompiro refugees sought haven far to the south in the recently established missions at El Paso. Others moved to the more densely populated and therefore more easily defended regions to the north, in the pueblos around Santa Fe.

Violence in the region appears to have subsided by the middle of the 1670s, but tensions throughout the pueblos remained high. Hispanic and Franciscan prestige stood at an all-time low in New Mexico. European colonial dominance, based precariously upon a dissolving Spanish presence in the land, now offered little but continued hardship. As Fray Francisco de Ayeta observed at the time, the province "was falling into utter ruin."[34]

Perhaps cognizant of the growing agitation among the Pueblos and eager to smother any spark of open rebellion, civil and ecclesiastical authorities in the province closed ranks and embarked on a policy of complete intolerance of the continued practice of Pueblo traditions. Under the governorship of Juan Francisco Treviño (1675–77), New Mexico's Indians suffered a level of persecution never seen before. Treviño outlawed Pueblo congregations in kivas

163

and ordered many of the subterranean ceremonial chambers destroyed.[35] Such steps were without precedent in the colony's seventy-five-year history and struck at the heart of Pueblo cultural identity.

Signs of the growing volatility of the situation appeared in 1675, when Treviño forced a direct confrontation with native leaders intent on protecting Pueblo values and traditions. At some point during that year the governor ordered the arrest, public whipping, and imprisonment in Santa Fe of forty-seven medicine men from pueblos across the province in reaction to rumors that some of the Pueblo sorcerers had bewitched Fray Andrés Durán and a number of his relatives. Treviño then ordered four of the prisoners publicly hanged. Three met that fate; the fourth committed suicide in his cell before the sentence could be carried out.

Enraged by the governor's brutality, the Pueblos acted. Seventy Pueblo warriors forced entry into Treviño's private quarters, threatening to kill the governor and his dependents and incite revolt unless he released the remaining medicine men immediately. Treviño yielded to the Indians' demands and let the prisoners go. In doing so he staved off certain rebellion, for a large force of Tewas had concealed themselves in the hills around Santa Fe, poised to attack if the governor did not agree to the ultimatum.[36]

Treviño's capitulation demonstrated the efficacy of concerted action to many Pueblos previously uncommitted to open defiance of colonial and Franciscan authority, edging the province ever closer toward widespread rebellion. The concept of revolt, however, was not new to the Pueblos. Violent uprisings, coupled with brutal suppressions by Hispanic overlords, had dotted the history of New Mexico since the colony's inception. The first Pueblo attempts at unifying the region's disparate language groups

for a united stand against the Hispanic presence had surfaced by mid-century. As one veteran Hispanic soldier,
Juan Domínguez de Mendoza, recounted in 1681,

> From the time of General Alonso Pacheco de Heredia
> [1642–44], during whose term he [Mendoza] entered this
> kingdom as a child of twelve years, he has seen fourteen
> señores governors who have governed this kingdom, and
> they have always taken action against the natives of all
> nations due to their idolatries and evil customs. He
> knows particularly that Don Fernando de Argüello in his
> time [1644–47] had twenty-nine Jemez Indians hanged in
> the pueblo of Los Jemez as traitors and confederates of
> the Apaches, and that he had imprisoned a number of
> them for the same crime and for having killed Diego
> Martínez Naranjo. And in the time of Señor General
> Hernando de Ugarte y la Concha [1649–53] there were
> hanged as traitors and confederates of the Apaches some
> [Tiwa] Indians of La Isleta and of the pueblos of La
> Alemeda, San Felipe, Cochití, and Jemez, nine from the
> said pueblos being hanged. The common people of this
> kingdom have always been punished as idolaters, and in
> particular in the time of Señor General Don Fernando de
> Villanueva [1665–68], in the province of Los Piros, some
> were hanged and burned in the pueblo of Senecú as
> traitors and sorcerers.[37]

The success of each of these attempts had hinged upon
the ability of resistance leaders to win widespread support
among a heterogeneous Pueblo populace while ensuring
that word of their activities did not reach members of the
European community via the treacherous ears of Hispanic
sympathizers within the native ranks. Some, like the Tiwa
plan of the early 1650s, failed as efforts to maintain secrecy
foundered. Others remained closely guarded secrets but
fell short of gaining a critical mass of support. Soon after

the failed Tiwa revolt, as one Keres native recounted in 1681, leaders from the pueblo of Taos

> sent through the pueblos of the custodia two deerskins with some pictures on them signifying conspiracy after their manner, in order to convoke the people to a new rebellion, and the said deerskins passed to the province of Moqui, where they refused to accept them. The pact [among the pueblos] which had been forming ceased for the time being, but they always kept in their hearts the desire to carry it out.[38]

Experience in planning these attempts at revolt soon taught resistance-minded Pueblos the importance of seeking out the cooperation of leaders in the Pueblo community who, in addition to responsibilities to their native towns, enjoyed positions of authority within the church and Spanish colonial hierarchy. Pivotal players in the dangerous game of conspiracy, such leaders were capable of mustering extensive support throughout the pueblos while using their status as mission officers or as liaisons with civil authorities to prevent word of an impending uprising from reaching the Hispanic community. Esteban Clemente, the Spanish-named Indian governor for all the pueblos of Las Salinas and a vocal supporter of the Franciscan cause during Mendizábal's legalization of the kachinas in the early 1660s, chose exactly this role in the ill-fated revolt of the southeastern pueblos during Governor Villanueva's administration (1665–68).[39] As one settler later told the story:

> Clemente, whom the whole kingdom secretly obeyed . . . formed a conspiracy which was general throughout the kingdom, giving orders to the Christian Indians that all the horse droves of all the jurisdictions should be driven to the sierras, in order to leave the Spaniards afoot; and

that on the night of Holy Thursday . . . they must destroy the whole body of Christians, not leaving a single
religious or Spaniard. This treason being discovered,
they hanged the said Indian, Don Esteban, and quieted
the rest.[40]

Any doubts about the executed leader's true allegiance
vanished during a search of his property, for "there was
found in his house a large number of idols and entire kettles
full of idolatrous powdered herbs, feathers, and other
trifles."[41] A decade and a half later, as Otermín led the
surviving Hispanics south after the successful uprising of
August 1680, many refugees noted bitterly that "the Indians who have done the greatest harm are those who have
been most favored by the religious and who are the most
intelligent."[42]

The lessons learned from these failed attempts at revolt
figured prominently in renewed preparations for an armed
uprising in the latter half of the 1670s. Despite the Treviño
incident of 1675 and its highlighting of the growing political instability in the region, church and colonial officials
continued to advocate a policy of unforgiving repression
against acts of nativism in the Pueblo community. Francisco Xavier, Treviño's secretary of government and war
and principle architect of the governor's harsh Indian
policy, continued to serve in the same capacity under
Governor Antonio de Otermín after his arrival in 1677. In
these years, Xavier's crackdown on Pueblo traditional
practices and beliefs and his unremitting persecution of
one medicine man in particular — Popé from the pueblo of
San Juan — committed unprecedented numbers of Pueblos
to the idea of violent rebellion and touched off the chain of
events that would culminate in the happenings of August
1680.[43]

The exact nature of Popé's role in the revolt of 1680, like many of the details of Pueblo preparations for the uprising, remains hidden in historical obscurity. One of the forty-three medicine men freed after the confrontation in Treviño's quarters in 1675, Popé continued to defy Spanish authority from his home in San Juan until threats from Xavier forced him to seek refuge among the Tiwas of Taos.[44] From that remote northern pueblo, tales gradually spread through Indian circles of how this medicine man communicated regularly with several of the key deities of Pueblo cosmology. As one Pueblo witness later told Spanish colonial authorities, these encounters took place in one of the Taos kivas, and at one point

> there appeared to the said Popé three figures of Indians who never came out of the estufa. They gave the said Popé to understand that they were going underground to the lake of Copala. He saw these figures emit fire from all the extremities of their bodies, and that one of them was called Caudi, another Tilini, and the other Theume; and these three beings spoke to the said Popé.[45]

The story continued that the three figures instilled Popé with a plan to revolt against Spanish rule and return his people to life as it was before the coming of the Europeans, "because the God of the Spaniards was worth nothing and theirs was very strong, the Spaniard's God being rotten wood."[46] Accordingly, in the summer of 1680, Popé began to coordinate plans for a general uprising.

Secrecy obsessed Popé in his preparations for the revolt. From his distant mountain kiva he dispatched runners, charged to secrecy under pain of death, to bring his message of liberation to every pueblo in the land. Slowly, a network of Pueblo leaders sympathetic to Popé's cause evolved that included the Tewa war chief of San Ildefonso,

Francisco El Ollita, the Keresan leader Antonio Malacate, Luis Tupatú of Picurís, and a host of other war chiefs and captains from Taos, San Lorenzo, Jemez, and Pecos. Significantly, the list of conspirators also included several prominent mestizos and other persons of mixed heritage, most notably Alonzo Catití of Santo Domingo, Nicolás Jonva of San Ildefonso, Domingo Romero from Tesuque, and Domingo Naranjo of Santa Clara.[47]

Fearful that the Spaniards might learn of their impending fate and smash yet another uprising in its infancy, the leaders chose the times and places of their meetings carefully, convening only during the saint's day festivals of pueblos sympathetic to their cause. In this way they hoped to avoid raising suspicions about the movement and congregation of so many important Pueblos at one time.[48] Popé at one point ordered the murder of his son-in-law, Nicolás Bua, upon the latter's discovery of the plans to rebel. As the Indian governor of San Juan, Bua's pro-Spanish sentiments were well known. His knowledge of the revolt posed a risk Popé could not take.[49]

By August 1680, the stage had been set. The movement's leaders chose August 12 as the date on which the revolt would take place, hoping to catch the Hispanic community at its weakest in the weeks before the arrival of the triennial supply caravan.[50] On August 9, Popé dispatched runners, each carrying a cord of knotted maguey fiber, and

> the cord was passed through all the pueblos of the kingdom so that the ones which agreed to it might untie one knot in sign of obedience, and by the other knots they would know the days which were lacking; and this was to be done on pain of death to those who refused to agree to it.[51]

Only the Piro pueblos in the south—for some reason

deemed untrustworthy—were excluded from the call to action.[52]

The word given, the Pueblos prepared to strike. But news of their intentions reached Otermín on August 9, when the leaders of San Marcos, San Cristóbal, and La Ciénega opted out of the rebellion and informed the governor of the impending revolt. Almost simultaneously, messages reached Otermín from two Franciscan friars in the province and the alcalde mayor at Taos confirming the rumors of a planned uprising. The governor responded swiftly, ordering maestre de campo Francisco Gómez Robledo to arrest two of Popé's messengers from the pueblo of Tesuque and bring them to Santa Fe for questioning.[53]

But the governor was now powerless to halt the momentum of Pueblo liberation. Robledo's actions warned the inhabitants of Tesuque that yet another carefully planned rebellion was in danger of being smothered under the weight of Spanish vigilance, and local leaders dispatched messengers across the province advancing the timetable for the revolt.[54] In the meantime, the people of Tesuque took steps of their own to push the movement forward, beginning with the murder on the night of August 9 of a resident Hispanic, Cristóbal de Herrera. And on the morning of Sunday, August 10, as Fray Juan Pío rode into the canyon outside Tesuque to meet the pueblo's fleeing inhabitants and his own death, more than eighty years of Pueblo fury fell upon New Mexico's Hispanic community.

Epilogue

As the stream of refugees led by Otermín reached El Paso del Norte in early October 1680, there was ample time for the Hispanic outcasts to reflect on the forces that had combined to extinguish their presence in New Mexico so effectively. Any thoughts the governor might have entertained of regrouping his forces and attempting an immediate reconquest of the confederated Pueblos quickly faded; the displaced settlers were keenly aware that a Spanish reentry into the province would only "give the Indians further cause to mock and scoff" at the tattered remains of New Mexico's once dominant Hispanic populace.[1]

Instead, the governor concentrated on holding his position on the northern border of Nueva Vizcaya. Poorly supplied, stripped of their possessions, and very conscious of their vulnerability should the wave of rebellion spread through the Indian groups around El Paso—Mansos, Janos, and Sumas—many of the settlers chafed to continue south to the safety of the interior of New Spain. A decree by the governor of Nueva Vizcaya, issued at Otermín's request, checked this impulse, expressly forbidding "for any cause, reasons, pretext, order, or excuse whatever, any person of whatever state, quality, or condition he may be, [to] pass from the said kingdom of New Mexico . . . except by permission and order of their governor, with whom they should remain until the most excellent señor viceroy shall decide and order otherwise." Violation of the decree carried an immediate and irrevocable sentence of death.[2]

Over the next twelve months, Otermín concentrated on fortifying his encampment and readying his forces to comply with the viceroy's order of January 1681 to retake the lost province at the earliest possible opportunity.[3] The task proved far from simple, as the governor received little in the way of reinforcements from the south and contended with overwhelming opposition among the members of his camp to the idea of returning north. Nevertheless, on November 5, 1681, Otermín set out on his mission of reconquest, leaving El Paso at the head of 146 soldiers, a scant 112 Piro, Manso, Jemez, and Tiwa auxiliaries, and a handful of friars under the leadership of Fray Francisco de Ayeta. A muster roll taken by the governor at El Ancón de Fray García three days later revealed the pitiful state of his force. Only twenty-five of the soldiers carried a complete set of arms and cavalry equipment, the others making do with little more than a dagger and shield.[4]

Over the next two months, Otermín's forces traveled throughout the Piro and southern Tiwa pueblos. An advance party led by Juan Domínguez de Mendoza reached as far north as the Keres pueblo of Cochití.[5] Otermín himself established a base camp among the southern Tiwas at Isleta, where, after a short round of initial hostilities, the town's five hundred inhabitants welcomed the returning Europeans as protection against a Tewa and northern Tiwa coalition bent on destroying the pueblo.

Elsewhere, however, the Pueblo reception was less amicable, as fear and uncertainty about the expedition's intentions permeated Indian circles. Word had spread quickly throughout the region that Francisco Xavier, hated architect of the persecution of Pueblo nativism in the years leading up to the revolt, was among those now returning to the land. Indeed, as Fray Nicolás López would later recount, when the expedition first entered Isleta many Indians watched in dismay while Xavier dismounted and "grabbed an Indian called Parraga by the hair and hurled him against the ground, beating and kicking him before most of the Spaniards," a scene that prompted the Pueblo witnesses to scream, "Why has that devil come? . . . already [Xavier is] beginning to do what he did before with the protection he had from the governor, for he used to do whatever he wished, and it was he [not Otermín] who governed."[6] As a result, Otermín's forces found each subsequent pueblo abandoned, its inhabitants having fled for fear of their former oppressors' wrath.

By January 1, 1682, signs were evident that a massive Pueblo contingent stood poised to attack the governor's forces. Judging the reconquest a failure, Otermín ordered his forces back to El Paso, accompanied by the now-alienated inhabitants of Isleta. Indications of the depth of Pueblo hatred for the Spanish and Franciscan yokes had been ubiquitous, as each pueblo's mission stood gutted and burned, each estancia looted. Weeks of effort had yielded only the most superficial reconciliations with those few

173

Pueblos encountered—and these most often were captives reasserting their loyalties to church and crown only under duress.

When interrogated, the captives painted vivid pictures of Pueblo efforts over the previous months to erase all memory of their years of contact with the Europeans. Many had followed Popé's instructions to wade into streams and scrub themselves with yucca root to wash away their Christian baptism. Still more had complied with orders sent out by the leader of the successful revolt that forbade Spanish ever again to be spoken in the land and called for all Pueblos to abandon their church-sanctioned spouses and return to the old ways of choosing their mates.[7]

Moreover, Otermín's interrogations provided the governor with extensive testimony about the motivations and planning that had underpinned the rebellion.[8] When pieced together with statements by other Pueblo prisoners taken during the fighting at Santa Fe and the retreat down the Rio Grande fifteen months earlier, the Pueblos' words shed considerable light on the roots and history of their grievances. Pedro Namboa, an eighty-year-old Tiwa who had witnessed the coming and going of every Spanish governor since the time of Oñate, had stressed the depth of Pueblo animosity toward their colonial overlords and the care with which native leaders had protected their traditional ways and beliefs over the generations:

> The resentment which all the Indians have in their hearts has been so strong, from the time this kingdom was discovered, because the religious and the Spaniards took away their idols and forbade their idolatries; they have inherited successively from their old men the things pertaining to their ancient customs, and he has heard this resentment spoken of since he was of an age to understand.[9]

174

Yet despite their successful uprising, many of the Pueblos somberly realized "that in the end the Spaniards must come and [re]gain the kingdom, because they [too] were sons of the land and had grown up with the natives."[10]

Time would eventually prove this prediction correct. Traditional rivalries soon resurfaced to splinter the coalition that had expelled the Europeans. Popé himself aggravated many of these old feuds and in the process demonstrated the indelible mark that more than three generations of Spanish rule had left upon Pueblo society. In the months following the revolt, the mystic declared himself leader of the diverse peoples of the Rio Grande basin, making tours of the region in the style of the deposed colonial governors and demanding each community's excess produce as tribute.[11] Popé's decrees grew increasingly reactionary, not only calling for the destruction of all signs of the former Spanish presence in the region but also forbidding the planting of any seeds introduced by the Europeans and demanding that his followers devote long hours to ceremonial practice. By the time of Otermín's arrival in November 1681, Luis Tupatú of Picurís had staged a successful coup against Popé, supplanting the medicine man as spokesman for the Pueblo confederation.[12] Tupatú was not averse to capitalizing on his newfound power; he and another leading figure in the revolt, Alonso Catití, laid claim to and divided all of the large herds of livestock left in the Taos region by the fleeing Hispanics.[13]

Infighting among the Pueblos deepened after Otermín's departure in early 1682, and a fresh outbreak of epidemic disease combined with renewed depredations by the region's Athapaskan groups to add considerably to the woes of the land. In July 1683, hints of major fractures within the Pueblo coalition reached Otermín's outpost at

175

El Paso when an emissary from Luis Tupatú attempted to downplay the Picurís leader's role in the revolt and extended Tupatú's invitation for the Europeans to return to their former colony.[14] Otermín, however, had by now generated animosity within an ever-widening circle of New Mexico refugees frustrated by the governor's leadership, which they perceived as weak and ineffectual, and angered at his persistent refusal to allow the settlers to press on to more hospitable regions to the south. Otermín could therefore do little to follow up on Tupatú's reported overture and instead prepared to hand the matter over to his replacement, now en route from Mexico City.

Domingo Jironza Petrís de Cruzate arrived in El Paso to assume governorship of New Mexico in August 1683. There he found conditions so desperate that any hope he may have had of carrying out the standing order to retake the lost province at the earliest possible moment soon vanished. Impoverished and discontented, most of the New Mexico refugees lived in near-squalid conditions in encampments scattered along both banks of the Rio Grande. There they struggled to subsist on the area's limited resources, in the process straining relations with the Manso Indian inhabitants of the region severely. Preoccupied with stabilizing the Spanish presence in El Paso and with carrying out orders to establish a presidio of fifty men at the settlement, Jironza managed to send only a small reconnaissance party north to investigate the Tupatú reports in November 1683. Led by Salvador Holguín, the party had barely reached the southern fringes of Pueblo lands when a skirmish with Apache raiders forced it to return to El Paso, convinced that a new entrada would find little welcome in northern New Mexico.[15] The retaking of the province would have to wait.

176

Efforts to mount an effective and well-supplied expedition to reestablish Spanish colonial authority in New Mexico faced serious obstacles in the years that followed. Little impetus for returning and confronting their Pueblo attackers existed among the dispossessed colonists, many of whom managed to sidestep the royal orders to remain in El Paso and start life anew in other places along the frontier.[16] At the same time, organizing and financing a large-scale expedition of reconquest was an expense the crown could ill afford, as authorities in Mexico City and Madrid grappled with crises that erupted across virtually the entire northern rim of the viceroyalty in the years after the revolt.

In 1680, the English began their long campaign of encroachment upon Florida by attacking and eventually overrunning the Spanish missions at Guale, less than one hundred miles north of St. Augustine.[17] By 1685, Spanish colonial officials had learned of Louis XIV's designs to establish a French presence at the mouth of the Mississippi River and of La Salle's ill-fated expedition to achieve that goal. Unaware of the explorer's death on the south Texas coast in March 1687, and fearful of the access to Spanish shipping lanes in the Gulf and to the mining territories of Nueva Vizcaya that such an outpost would give the French, authorities in New Spain launched eleven expeditions—six overland from northeastern Mexico and five by sea—to apprehend La Salle between 1685 and 1689.[18] Meanwhile, the most serious threat to the security of the viceroyalty gathered steam along the northern frontier itself. Hoping to build on the recent Pueblo successes and rid their lands of unwanted Europeans, Manso, Jano, Suma, Taboso, Julime, Concha, and Pima Indians staged separate uprisings of their own beginning at various times after 1684, spreading violence over an area extending from Sonora to Coahuila.[19]

Consequently, while the crown remained committed to the idea of an eventual return to New Mexico for both strategic and evangelical reasons, for the moment royal attentions focused on solidifying the Spanish position at El Paso and on extinguishing the flames of rebellion that threatened to engulf the entire northern frontier. Any attempted foray into New Mexico would receive little in the way of financial backing from the royal treasury, a fact stressed by Charles II in royal cédulas of September 4, 1683, and September 13, 1689: a new entrada would be undertaken only "with the greatest economy possible to my royal treasury."[20]

In the meantime, the presidio at El Paso and its personnel became key elements in the Spanish campaign to smother Indian uprisings as they erupted across northern Nueva Vizcaya, Sonora, and Sinaloa. From the spring of 1684 onward, forces from the garrison repeatedly answered calls from neighboring settlements for help in combating Indian insurgents.[21] And while both Pedro Reneros de Posada, governor of New Mexico from 1686 to 1689, and Jironza, serving a second term from 1689 to 1691, managed to lead reconnaissance expeditions into northern New Mexico during their respective terms, neither accomplished more than the quick brutalization of the inhabitants of the pueblos they entered before returning to El Paso. As a result, their forays did little to further the Spanish aim of resettling the province and only heightened Pueblo animosity toward their former overlords.[22]

The successful recolonization of New Mexico resulted from the efforts of Jironza's successor, Diego de Vargas Zapata Luján Ponce de León.[23] Boasting one of the more prominent lineages on the Iberian peninsula, and eager to rise above the middle administrative posts in which he had served effectively since his arrival in New Spain in 1673, Vargas secured an appointment as governor of New Mexico by viceregal decree on September 25, 1690.

By this time, momentum had begun to build for a full-scale resettlement of the northern province. Jironza, encouraged by his 1689 journey up the Rio Grande, had laid plans for a major entrada in the spring of 1690 when yet another outbreak of Indian hostilities to the southwest forced the governor to commit his resources to the relief of Casas Grandes. Further campaigning in the region occupied Jironza's attention for the remainder of the year. In the meantime, royal officials in Mexico City and Madrid listened attentively to a petition by Toribio de la Huerta, a former New Mexico colonist, who offered to finance his own expedition of reconquest in exchange for generous land grants, various noble and military titles, and rights to production at potential mercury and silver mines that de la Huerta claimed to have discovered west of the Hopi pueblos in the years preceding the revolt.[24] But Vargas's own offer to finance the resettlement and his more favorable standing in royal circles won him preference as the person to lead the effort to retake New Mexico. He took office in El Paso on February 22, 1691, hoping to proceed with the project at the earliest possible moment.[25]

Full appreciation of the poverty of the settlement at El Paso and the continuing demands placed on the presidio's forces in the campaign against hostile Indian groups on the Sonora frontier checked the new governor's optimism and delayed the proposed expedition. Still, Vargas had reason to hope for a successful outcome to his New Mexico venture once given free reign to proceed. The viceroy approved the governor's request that his expedition be augmented with fifty additional *presidarios* drawn from

Nueva Vizcaya, Sonora, and Sinaloa upon completion of the latest Sonoran campaign. Also, Mexico City continued to express interest in the rumors sparked by de la Huerta of rich mercury and silver deposits west of the Hopi pueblos. Vargas actively encouraged that interest in his correspondence with royal officials throughout 1691 and into 1692, well aware that all parties concerned agreed that a proper investigation of the reports could only be made from a reoccupied Santa Fe.

In addition, captives taken during Jironza's 1689 incursion into the lost province continued to report an almost total breakdown of the Pueblo unity that had fueled the success of the revolt almost a decade before. In 1688, inhabitants of the Tewa pueblos and Picurís had deposed Luis Tupatú, and Popé had arisen once again to prominence. Refusing to acknowledge the medicine man's leadership, however, the people of Jemez, Taos, and Pecos joined with the Keres at Cochití, Santa Ana, Zía, San Felipe, and Santo Domingo to wage open warfare against their former allies. Hostilities had flared between the Zuñis and the people of the Hopi pueblos, and raids by surrounding Apache and Ute bands continued without mercy across the region. Fractures within specific pueblos had also appeared: contingents from Acoma, Zía, and Santa Ana had broken away from their communities to form a joint settlement at Laguna.[26]

Vargas recognized all too well the potential for capitalizing on the deteriorating state of affairs among the Pueblos. When he was at last able to begin his mission of reconquest beginning in August 1692, the governor was eager to work the tensions and sufferings in the region to his advantage. As he led an extensive reconnaissance of the province during the fall of 1692, Vargas avoided the iron-fisted tactics of his recent predecessors. With overtures of peace and carefully crafted diplomacy, he won pledges of renewed loyalty and adherence to the Christian faith from the leaders of twenty-three pueblos before returning to El Paso before the end of the year.[27]

While he prepared to carry out the second phase of his mission—the actual resettlement of the province—Vargas benefited from the wave of excitement that reports of his bloodless and hitherto self-financed reconquest of New Mexico had generated in Mexico City. With an official letter of gratitude from the viceroy and a grant of forty thousand pesos from the royal treasury, the governor gathered a force of one hundred soldiers, seventy families, an unspecified number of Indian auxiliaries, and eighteen Franciscan friars and struck north for Santa Fe on October 4, 1693.

Reentering the province for the second time, Vargas quickly learned that the conciliatory gestures made to the Spaniards by many Pueblo factions the year before had been feigned. Determined resistance awaited the governor's attempt to reestablish a permanent colonial authority in the province. Only four pueblos—Santa Ana, Zia, San Felipe, and Pecos—showed signs of honoring their pledges from the previous year and a willingness to accept a renewed European presence in New Mexico, and even these communities suffered internal dissent over the issue.[28]

The first confrontation came in late December, as the Tewas and Tanos who had taken up residence in Santa Fe during the Spaniards' absence refused to surrender the villa to Vargas. After two weeks of failed negotiations and the deaths of twenty-two of his followers from exposure to a bitter year-end snow, Vargas abandoned diplomacy and ordered the attack. Supported by one hundred forty re-

181

cently arrived warriors from Pecos, the governor's forces took Santa Fe on December 30. One Spaniard and nine of the Pueblos who had chosen to resist Vargas's demands died in the fighting. The governor oversaw the execution of seventy Indians captured during and after the battle on charges of treason and apostatasy, while the remainder of the prisoners—numbering about four hundred—received sentences of ten years of servitude. The words of those Pueblos who had warned of the brutality that would surely accompany the Spaniards' return had proven only too prophetic.

Establishing control over the province and either sub-duing or driving off those Pueblo factions that rejected a return to colonial rule occupied Vargas for the next three years. After recapturing Santa Fe, the governor spent most of 1694 directing the military campaign to silence Pueblo opposition to the Spanish resettlement. It was a year that saw the return of an old and familiar pattern: with supplies dwindling and no crops of their own yet established, the colonists relied for survival on stores of maize and livestock taken forcibly from the pueblos during raids or plundered after the Indians had abandoned their homes and fled to the surrounding mountains to escape Spanish abuse. The ar-rival of 230 additional settlers in June only worsened this stress on communities whose agricultural cycles had al-ready suffered months of violent dislocation.

By the fall of 1694 much of the fighting had ended, and Vargas had established tenuous authority over the province with the exception of Taos and Picurís to the north and Zuñi, Acoma, and the Hopi pueblos to the west. In the following year the Franciscans accompanying Vargas rees-tablished missions in eleven of the pueblos surrounding Santa Fe. At the same time, the governor chose settlement sites and distributed land to colonists whose numbers were augmented yet again with the arrival of forty-four additional families on May 9, 1695.

A harsh winter in 1695–96 stoked Pueblo discontent, however, as Spanish demands for precious livestock and grain only intensified. Many of the communities closest to Spanish areas of settlement—particularly the Tewa pueblos of San Juan, San Ildefonso, Santa Clara, Pojoaque, Nambé, and Tesuque—saw their best lands taken away by the governor and given to the families who had followed him up the Rio Grande.[29] By December 1695, Franciscans stationed in the outlying missions had received strong indications that plans for a rebellion of the scope of that executed some sixteen years before circulated once again among the Pueblos. The priests' repeated warnings to Vargas of impending violence were finally fulfilled on June 4, 1696, when five missionaries and twenty-one settlers lost their lives in a coordinated uprising that threatened to repeat the Pueblo successes of 1680.[30]

From its inception, however, the rebellion lacked the widespread support and unity that had fired the earlier Pueblo victory. Leaders at Pecos, Tesuque, San Felipe, Santa Ana, and Zía maintained their loyalty to Vargas, and warrior auxiliaries from these towns played a crucial role in the governor's successful campaign to quash the revolt over the next six months. More importantly, the war chiefs and medicine men who led the armed campaign to oust the Europeans did so without the unified support of their own communities. Weary of the cycle of violence, dislocation, starvation, and hardship that yet another show of resistance promised, many inhabitants of the pueblos at the center of this latest outbreak of fighting dreaded the chain of events they now faced once again.

183

In San Cristóbal, for example, a Tano woman recounted the killing of two friars in the village on the first day of the uprising and told of how "the old Indian women and other women put their arms around [the bodies] and wept over them tenderly, sorrowful over the death of the said two religious and lamenting the hardships which they expected to undergo in the mountains with their children." She noted also that "some of the Indian men were of this same sentiment."[31] Without broad-based support across the province, many of the participants in the uprising who were not killed or captured by Vargas's forces during the ensuing campaigns fled, taking up residence in the far western pueblos or among surrounding Athapaskan groups.[32] By the end of the year, the last overt Pueblo effort to rid New Mexico of Spanish colonial rule had ended.

The turn of the eighteenth century in New Mexico brought with it a dramatic change in the course of Pueblo-Spanish relations that would carry the province through to the end of the colonial period. In the generations after Vargas's reconquest, toleration and cooperation to a degree unimaginable in the previous century underscored the interaction of the two peoples.[33] Depredations beginning as early as 1706 by Comanche groups newly arrived in New Mexico added to the ongoing threat posed by the region's Athapaskans and galvanized a military alliance within the colony that saw Pueblo warriors cooperate closely with— and often outnumber—colonial militia in campaigns against the raiders.[34] Recognizing the importance of that cooperation to the defense of the province, and hoping to avoid a resurfacing of the tensions that had sparked rebellion in 1680, colonial officials moderated the demands placed upon their Pueblo vassals. The encomienda never reappeared in New Mexico in the eighteenth century, and tribute requirements seem to have been significantly reduced from their pre-revolt levels.[35] At the same time, missionary activity in the region lost much of the zeal that had threatened Pueblo ways and generated the antagonisms of the seventeenth century. Franciscans in New Mexico now operated within a province where matters of defense often took precedence over evangelization.[36]

Over the course of the eighteenth and early nineteenth centuries, this atmosphere of reduced tensions between native and nonaboriginal segments of New Mexican society allowed the Pueblos to continue relatively unfettered in their attempts to preserve traditional ways and beliefs. In the far west, the Hopi pueblos remained independent for the remainder of the colonial period, their inhabitants never again swearing allegiance to the church and the Spanish crown. Together with the region's surrounding nomadic bands, these communities served as a haven for refugees from pueblos in proximity to the European settlements who chose to reject all contact with the colonists. Pueblo inhabitants of the Rio Grande basin who opted not to flee their communities met only minimal persecution from church and colonial authorities for acts of nativism. At the same time, the leaders of these communities became adept at working within the colonial system to protect Pueblo land and legal rights against encroachments by profit-minded settlers.[37]

Still, as tension and animosity between Pueblos and Hispanics slowly gave way to familiarity and close interaction, change inevitably worked its way into the daily lives of the land's oldest inhabitants. Demographic shifts in the province did much to facilitate the incorporation of European ways into Pueblo societies. New Mexico's Indian population continued to suffer losses from disease, warfare, and migration to regions beyond Spanish control. As a result, the number of Pueblos within colonial jurisdiction never rose above ten thousand during the eighteenth century.[38] In the meantime, the Hispanic population grew steadily in the generations after the reconquest. At mid-century, non-Indian settlers outstripped the Pueblos with whom they shared the province, and by 1810 Hispanics outnumbered Pueblos in the colony by two to one.[39]

The steadily growing presence of Hispanics in New Mexico inevitably brought change—biological, social, and cultural—to the Pueblos with whom they came into contact on an increasingly intimate basis. Miscegenation continued to erase the genetic lines separating the land's native inhabitants from the newest set of colonists for the remainder of the colonial period.[40] And while the Pueblos' understanding and effective exploitation of legal, political, and commercial relations within the Spanish system did much to protect their communities and their way of life from European encroachment, the Indians' acceptance of and eventual reliance upon that system to serve their needs inexorably tied them into the colonial structure to a degree not seen in the generations before the revolt.[41]

Finally, the less confrontational nature of the Franciscan missionary effort and the emigration of Pueblos more staunchly opposed to European ways facilitated a more liberal interchange of customs, superstitions, and beliefs within the colony. Spanish Catholic precepts penetrated Pueblo worldviews more effectively—or at least to a more lasting degree—than in the decades before the revolt, eventually yielding the distinctly New Mexican interpretations of Christianity practiced in many pueblos today.[42] Thus, the daily lives of Pueblo Indians and European settlers intertwined with increasing intricacy over the remainder of the colonial period in New Mexico, weaving the two peoples together into the complex tapestry that represents New Mexico's colonial heritage.

Notes

Preface

1. Elizabeth A. H. John, "A View from the Spanish Borderlands," *Proceedings of the American Antiquarian Society* 101:1 (1991), p. 80 (hereafter cited as "View"). As a professor of history at Harvard University in the late nineteenth century, Francis Parkman (1823–93) penned a number of works renowned for their rich narratives and captivating descriptions of the history of colonial North America.

2. See, for example, Elizabeth A. H. John, *Storms Brewed in Other Men's Worlds: The Confrontation of Indians, Spanish, and French in the Southwest, 1540–1795*; Ramón A. Gutiérrez's controversial work *When Jesus Came the Corn Mothers Went Away: Marriage, Sexuality, and Power in New Mexico, 1500–1846*; and David J. Weber's important overview of the Borderlands in the colonial period, *The Spanish Frontier in North America* (hereafter cited as *Storms*, *Corn Mothers*, and *Spanish Frontier*, respectively.)

3. See Herbert E. Bolton, "Need for Publication of a

Comprehensive Body of Documents Relating to the History of Spanish Activities within the Present Limits of the United States," in John F. Bannon, ed., *Bolton and the Spanish Borderlands*, pp. 23–31.

4. The two most detailed interpretations along this line can be found in Edward Spicer, *Cycles of Conquest: The Impact of Spain, Mexico, and the United States on the Indians of the Southwest, 1533–1960* (hereafter cited as *Cycles of Conquest*); and Van Hastings Garner, "Seventeenth Century New Mexico," *Journal of Mexican-American Studies* 4 (1974), pp. 41–70. Similar stances are held by John in *Storms* and Gutiérrez in *Corn Mothers*.

5. See, for instance, Charles Wilson Hackett's introduction to *Revolt of the Pueblo Indians of New Mexico and Otermín's Attempted Reconquest, 1680–1682* (hereafter cited as *Revolt*); and Jack Forbes, *Apache, Navajo, and Spaniard*.

6. France V. Scholes, "Civil Government and Society in New Mexico in the Seventeenth Century," *New Mexico Historical Review* 10:2 (April 1935), pp. 71–111 (hereafter cited as "Civil Government and Society").

7. Robert Coles, *The Call of Stories: Teaching and the Moral Imagination*, p. 204.

8. John, "View," p. 86.

Prologue

1. *Auto* of Otermín, Santa Fe, August 9, 1680, in Hackett, *Revolt* 1:3.

2. Ibid. 1:5.

3. Declaration of Pedro Hidalgo, Soldier, Santa Fe, August 10, 1680, *Revolt* 1:7. Joe S. Sando reports that *el opi* (El Obi) was a general term adapted by the Spaniards from *opi*, the Tanoan title of War Chief.

4. Petition of Fray Francisco de Ayeta, Mexico, May 10, 1679, in *Historical Documents Relating to New Mexico, Nueva Vizcaya, and Approaches Thereto, to 1773*, ed. Charles Wilson Hackett, 3 vols., 3:299 (hereafter cited as *Documents*).

5. Auto, Santa Fe, August 10, 1680, *Revolt* 1:7.

6. Judicial Process and Declaration, Santa Fe, August 10, 1680, and August 13–20, 1680, *Revolt* 1:9, 12.

7. Auto, Santa Fe, August 10, 1680, *Revolt* 1:7.

8. Ibid. 1:8; and Certification of August 10, 1680, *Revolt* 1:8.

9. Judicial Process and Declaration, August 10, 1680, *Revolt* 1:8–9.

10. Auto and Declaration of *Maestre de Campo* Francisco Gómez, Santa Fe, August 12, 1680, *Revolt* 1:10.

11. Auto, Santa Fe, August 13, 1680, *Revolt* 1:11.

12. Ibid.

13. Ibid.

14. Auto and Judicial Process, August 13–20, 1680, *Revolt* 1:13.

15. Ibid.

16. Ibid. 1:14.

17. Ibid.

18. Auto, Santa Fe, August 21, 1680, *Revolt* 1:18.

19. Auto and Judicial Process, Santa Fe, August 13–20, 1680, *Revolt* 1:14.

20. Ibid. 1:15.

21. Otermín to Ayeta, September 8, 1680, *Revolt* 1:101.

22. Auto and Judicial Process, Santa Fe, August 13–20, 1680, *Revolt* 1:15.

23. Ibid.

24. Auto, Santa Fe, August 21, 1680, *Revolt* 1:17.

25. Ibid. 1:17–18.

26. Certification and Notice of Departure, Santa Fe, August 21, 1680, *Revolt* 1:19.

27. Auto of the March and Halting Places, August 24–26, 1680, *Revolt* 1:22; and Continuation of Otermín's March, August 26, 1680, *Revolt* 1:26.

28. Ibid. 1:27.

29. Ibid.

30. Order of the Arrest . . . of the Lt. General, Alonso García, El Alamillo, September 6, 1680, *Revolt* 1:63.

31. Autos of Alonso García, La Isleta, August 14, 1680, and El Socorro, August 24, 1680, *Revolt* 1:65–80.

32. Auto of Otermín, September 6, 1680, *Revolt* 1:84.

33. Reply of the *Fiscal*, Mexico, January 7, 1681, *Revolt* 2:231.

34. Auto de Junta de Guerra, La Salineta, October 2, 1680, *Revolt* 1:161.

35. Ayeta to the Viceroy, El Paso, September 11, 1680, *Revolt* 1:107.

Part I

1. See Marc Simmons, "History of Pueblo-Spanish Relations to 1821," in Alfonso Ortíz, ed., *Handbook of North American Indians, Volume 9: The Southwest,* p. 179 (hereafter cited as *Handbook*, with appropriate volume number).

Chapter 1

1. The Appointment of Don Juan de Oñate as Governor and Captain General of New Mexico, October 21, 1595, *Don Juan de Oñate, Colonizer of New Mexico, 1595–1628,* ed. and trans. George P. Hammond and Agapito Rey, 2 vols., 1:59–63 (hereafter cited as *Oñate*).

2. For the journey of Cabeza de Vaca and his three companions—Andrés Dorantes, his black slave Estevanico, and Alonso de Castillo Maldonado—see *La Relación o Naufragios de Alvar Núñez Cabeza de Vaca* (1542), ed. Martín A. Favata y José B. Fernández, particularly chapters 30 and 31, pp. 114–121 (hereafter cited as *Relación*). Unfortunately, the exact point at which Cabeza de Vaca and company crossed the Río Grande remains unknown.

3. The most authoritative works on the oft-told story of the de Niza and Coronado expeditions remain Herbert E. Bolton's *Coronado on the Turquoise Trail: Knight of Pueblos and Plains,* and George P. Hammond's edited and translated collection of relevant documents contained in *Narratives of the Coronado Expedition, 1540–1542* (hereafter cited as *Narratives*), from which the

following narrative passages are drawn. See also John, *Storms,* pp. 13–23.

4. Report of Fray Marcos de Niza, in Hammond, *Narratives,* p. 79.

5. See *Colección de documentos inéditos relativos al descubrimiento, conquista, y organización de las antiguas posesiones de América y Oceana,* vol. 16 (Madrid, 1871), pp. 142–187; and George P. Hammond and Agapito Rey, eds. and trans., *The Rediscovery of New Mexico, 1580–1594: The Explorations of Chamuscado, Espejo, Castaño de Sosa, Morlete, and Leyva de Bonilla and Humaña,* p. 6 (hereafter cited as *Rediscovery*).

6. For a thorough discussion of the roots and manifestations of Franciscan evangelism in New Mexico, see Gutiérrez, *Corn Mothers,* pp. 46, 55–94. Gutiérrez goes so far as to state that "from 1581 to 1680, Franciscans provided the impetus for colonization in New Mexico. For most of this period the friars were virtual lords of the land" (p. 46.) While partially correct, this stance neglects the strong emphasis placed by the crown upon northern expansion as a means to preempt encroachments upon Spanish territories by other European powers on the continent (see Thomas D. Hall, *Social Change in the Southwest, 1350–1880,* pp. 74–76; hereafter cited as *Social Change*) and, at a more local level, the personal ambitions of colonists and colonial officials bent upon making their fortunes in the northern land. In the seventeenth century, these ambitions would frequently place the nonreligious community in New Mexico in direct confrontation with the Franciscans (see chapter 5).

7. Hammond and Rey, *Rediscovery,* p. 9.

8. The best surviving account of the Chamuscado-Rodríguez expedition is Hernán Gallegos's *Relación* of 1582, reprinted in *Rediscovery,* pp. 67–114.

9. Hammond and Rey, *Rediscovery,* pp. 15–28; and George P. Hammond and Agapito Rey, eds. and trans., *Expedition into New Mexico Made by Antonio de Espejo, 1582–1583, As Revealed in the Journal of Diego Pérez de Luxán, a Member of the Party*

(hereafter cited as *Journal*).

10. Hammond and Rey, *Rediscovery*, pp. 15–28; Hammond and Rey, *Journal*.

11. Hammond and Rey, *Rediscovery*, pp. 28–50. Word of the fate of the Leyva expedition reached Spanish officials by way of a Mexican Indian who survived the attack and took up residence among the Tewas of the Rio Grande valley, where Oñate interviewed the survivor in 1599. See "Account Given by an Indian of the Flight of Leyva and Humaña from New Mexico, February 16, 1599," in *Rediscovery*, pp. 323–26.

12. Report of Alarcón's Expedition, in Hammond, *Narratives*, p. 145; and Castañeda's History of the Expedition, in Hammond and Rey, *Rediscovery*, p. 199.

13. Hammond, *Narratives*, p. 145; Hammond and Rey, *Rediscovery*, p. 199.

14. Hammond, *Narratives*, p. 17; John, *Storms*, p. 15.

15. Castañeda's History of the Expedition, *Narratives*, p. 224. Coronado himself denied such mistreatment of the Pueblos when called on to testify in defense of the actions of his men in 1544, claiming that the Indians had received fair payment for all of the goods taken from them. See Testimony of Francisco Vásquez de Coronado on the Management of the Expedition, September 3, 1544, *Narratives*, pp. 329–30.

16. Hammond, *Narratives*, p. 22 n. 68. For a discussion of Pueblo concepts of gifting and reciprocity, see Gutiérrez, *Corn Mothers*, pp. 8–17, 52.

17. Hammond and Rey, *Rediscovery*, p. 11.

18. *Gallegos' Relation of the Chamuscado-Rodríguez Expedition*, chap. 13, reprinted in *Rediscovery*, pp. 95–99.

19. Pérez de Lúxan, *Journal*, p. 116.

20. Report of the Exploratory Expedition to New Mexico Undertaken on July 27, 1590, by Gaspar Castaño de Sosa While He Was Lieutenant Governor and Captain General of Nueva León, *Rediscovery*, pp. 270–75.

21. Ibid. 1:59.

22. Viceroy to the King, November 15, 1596, in Hammond and Rey, *Oñate* 1:184.

23. Brief and True Account of the Discovery of New Mexico by Nine Men Who Set Out from Santa Bárbara in the Company of Three Franciscan Friars, *Rediscovery*, p. 142.

24. Advantages and Disadvantages of the Modifications of the Contract, Undated, *Oñate* 1:598.

25. The Appointment of Don Juan de Oñate as Governor and Captain General of New Mexico, October 21, 1595, *Oñate* 1:62; and Audiencia — Reasons for Supporting Oñate, November 15, 1595, *Oñate* 1:191.

26. *Oñate* 1:7; and Contract of Oñate, September 21, 1595, Ibid. 1:57.

27. Instructions to Oñate, October 21, 1595, *Oñate* 1:66; and Viceroy to the King, October 4, 1599, *Oñate* 1:502.

28. Monterrey to the King, May 4, 1598, *Oñate* 1:392.

29. Instructions to Oñate, October 21, 1595, *Oñate* 1:68.

30. Contract of Oñate, September 21, 1595, *Oñate* 1:43.

31. Salazar Inspection, December 22, 1597, *Oñate* 1:215–308.

32. Monterrey to the King, May 4, 1598, *Oñate* 1:390; Act of Taking Possession, April 30, 1598, *Oñate* 1:381; and John, *Storms*, p. 40.

33. Relaciones de todas las cosas que en el Nuevo México se han visto y sabido, asi por mar como por tierra desde el año 1538 hasta el de 1626 . . , por Fr. Gerónimo de Zárate Salmerón, *Documentos para servir a la historia de Nuevo México, 1583–1778*, ed. José Porrua Turanzas (Madrid, 1962), pp. 162–63.

34. Itinerary of the Expedition, in Hammond and Rey, *Oñate* 1:318; and Alfonso Ortíz, "San Juan Pueblo," in *Handbook* 9:281.

35. Fray Escobar's Diary, *Oñate* 2:1012.

36. The Valverde Investigation, Ortega Testimony, *Oñate* 2:661.

37. Act of Obedience and Vassalage by the Indians of San Juan Bautista, September 9, 1598, *Oñate* 1:342.

38. Gutiérrez, *Corn Mothers*, pp. 47–50; John, *Storms*, p. 43.

39. Translations were made by two men referred to only as the Mexican Indians Tomás and Cristóbal. One of them had been a member of the Castaño de Sosa expedition in 1590 and had remained behind in the pueblo of Santo Domingo; he translated from respective Pueblo languages to Nahua. The other translated from Nahua to Spanish. Act of Obedience and Vassalage by the Indians of Santo Domingo, July 7, 1598, *Oñate* 1:338; John, *Storms*, pp. 41–42.

40. Ibid. 1:338.

41. Trial of the Indians of Acoma, Testimony of Captain Villagrá, February 11, 1599, *Oñate* 1:428.

Chapter 2

1. Trial of the Indians of Acoma, Testimony of Captain Villagrá, February 11, 1599, in Hammond and Rey, *Oñate* 1:471; and Albert H. Schroeder, "Pueblos Abandoned in Historic Times," in *Handbook* 9:246.

2. Hernando de Alvarado, one of Coronado's lieutenants, was the first European to describe Acoma's cisterns in 1540. Members of the Antonio de Espejo expedition provided the first accounts of the Acomas' irrigation capabilities after his visit to the site in 1582. See Velma García-Mason, "Acoma Pueblo," in *Handbook* 9:455–56; Castañeda's history of the Coronado expedition reprinted in Hammond, *Narratives*, p. 218; and Pérez de Luxán, *Journal*, p. 35.

3. Relación del succeso, 1541, *Narratives*, p. 288.

4. Relation and Report of the Expedition Made by Francisco Sánchez Chamuscado and Eight Soldier Companions in the Exploration of New Mexico, in Hammond and Rey, *Rediscovery*, p. 107.

5. Trial of the Indians of Acoma, Testimony of Gerónimo Márquez, December 29, 1598, in Hammond and Rey, *Oñate* 1:431.

6. Ibid.; and Testimony of Gaspar López Tabora, December 29, 1598, *Oñate* 1:434.

7. Trial of the Indians of Acoma, Testimony of Gerónimo Márquez, December 29, 1598, in Hammond and Rey, *Oñate* 1:431; and Testimony of Juan Blazquez de Cabanillas, *Oñate* 1:446.

8. Hammond and Rey, *Oñate* 1:445–47.

9. Elizabeth A. John argues to the contrary, pointing out that turkeys were sacred to the Keresan inhabitants of the pueblo and hypothesizing that the violence at Acoma centered on a dispute between one of Zaldívar's men and a woman of the pueblo over one of the birds (see *Storms*, pp. 10–21).

10. Trial of the Indians of Acoma, Márquez, Tabora, de las Casas, and Zapata Testimonies, December 29, 1598, *Oñate* 1:430–41.

11. Statement of the Indian Caoma, February 9, 1599, *Oñate* 1:464.

12. Trial of the Indians of Acoma, Instructions to the Sargento Mayor, *Oñate* 1:456.

13. Ibid.

14. Ibid.; and Testimony of Bernabé de las Casas, *Oñate* 1:439.

15. Trial of the Indians of Acoma, Instructions to the Sargento Mayor, *Oñate* 1:456; Testimony of Captain Gerónimo Márquez, *Oñate* 1:433.

16. Trial of the Indians of Acoma, Instructions to the Sargento Mayor, *Oñate* 1:456; General Junta, *Oñate* 1:456.

17. Hammond and Rey, *Oñate* 1:433.

18. Ibid.; and Instructions to the Sargento Mayor, *Oñate* 1:456.

19. Members of the Chamuscado Rodríguez expedition staged a similar display of Franciscan benevolence during the 1581 Malajón uprising. See Gutiérrez, *Corn Mothers*, p. 58; and Hernán Gallegos' Relation of the Chamuscado-Rodriguéz Expedition, in Hammond and Rey, *Rediscovery*, p. 98.

20. Ibid. 1:458.

21. Ibid.; and Proceedings at Acoma, *Oñate* 1:461.

197

22. Hammond and Rey, *Oñate* 1:460.

23. Gaspar Pérez de Villagrá, *History of New Mexico* (1610), trans. Gilberto Espinosa, p. 228.

24. Trial of the Indians of Acoma, Proceedings at Acoma, *Oñate* 1:461.

25. Alonso Sánchez to Rodrigo del Río, February 28, 1599, *Oñate* 1:426.

26. Trial of the Indians of Acoma, Testimony of *Alférez* Vitorio Carbajal, *Oñate* 1:473.

27. Alonso Sánchez to Rodrigo del Río, February 28, 1599, *Oñate* 1:426.

28. Trial of the Indians of Acoma, Sentence, February 12, 1599, *Oñate* 1:477.

29. Little survives to illuminate the nature of these acts of resistance, which centered on the pueblos of Abó and Jumanos. See *Oñate*, p. 22–23; and Simmons, "History of Pueblo-Spanish Relations to 1821," in *Handbook* 9:181.

30. Oñate to the Viceroy, March 2, 1599, *Oñate* 1:487.

31. Captain Velasco to the Viceroy, San Gabriel, March 22, 1601, *Oñate* 2:608–18. This is evident both in Velasco's reference to the charge that the viceroy had placed upon him as the expedition prepared to depart (p. 609) and in his statement that "I am incurring no slight danger in giving your lordship such a detailed report of events in this land. For, however secret a thing may be, they make such investigations, both here and in Mexico, that I fear they will learn that I have written" (p. 618).

32. The Valverde Investigation, Horta Testimony, July 30, 1601, *Oñate* 2:656.

33. Proceedings of the Lt. Governor of New Mexico with Regard to Breaking Camp, San Gabriel, September 7, 1601, *Oñate* 2:672–89; and Francisco de Sosa Peñalosa to the Count of Monterrey, San Gabriel, October 1, 1601, *Oñate* 2:690–91.

34. Río de Losa to the Viceroy, January 13, 1602, *Oñate* 2:765.

35. Fray Juan de Escalona to His Prelate, October 1, 1601, *Oñate* 2:700.

36. Governor Oñate to the Viceroy, San Gabriel, August 24, 1607, *Oñate* 2:1044.

37. Discussion and Proposal of the Points Referred to His Majesty Concerning the Various Discoveries of New Mexico, *Oñate* 2:912.

38. Memorial of Fray Francisco de Velasco, April 9, 1609, *Oñate* 2:1095.

39. Ibid.

40. Appointment of an Agent to Report to the Viceroy on the Situation in New Mexico, Baca, Romero, Montesinos, and Hernández Testimonies, San Gabriel, October 2, 1601, *Oñate* 2:708, 711, 716, 719.

41. Governor Oñate to the Viceroy, San Gabriel, August 24, 1607, *Oñate* 2:1044.

42. New Mexico to be Maintained, January 29, 1609, *Oñate* 2:1077.

43. Royal Order Addressed to Don Juan de Oñate . . . Accepting His Resignation, Mexico, February 27, 1608, *Oñate* 2:1048.

44. Instructions to Don Pedro de Peralta, March 30, 1609, *Oñate* 2:1089.

45. Oñate to the King, April 7, 1599, *Oñate* 1:492.

Part II

1. This so-called "Spiritual Conquest" school of thought derives from Robert Ricard's landmark work, *La "Conquête Sprituelle" du Mexique* (1933). This model worked on the assumption that Spanish military successes undermined popular faith in local cosmologies at the time of contact, in a sense wiping clean the precontact slate of native religion. With their established belief systems erased, the indigenous peoples of newly conquered areas quickly and eagerly accepted the teachings of the Christian faith. Proponents of this line of thought contended that active resistance to missionary teachings was for the most part insignificant—any lack of enthusiasm on the part of the new

followers of the faith derived from an inertia, or "laziness," intrinsic to newly converted natives. Although these writers acknowledged the existence of "superstition" and variant local practices alongside Spanish missionizing efforts, they argued that these practices in no way indicated a persistence of precontact religious beliefs. For Ricard, such local practices were better understood as products of confusion or misunderstanding on the part of "ignorant" Indian neophytes whose unorthodox methods of worship derived from a twisted interpretation of Christian doctrine. In this, little separated the idiosyncratic Catholicism exhibited in Indian worship from the folk religion practiced in many European peasant communities. Refer to Nancy M. Farriss, *Maya Society Under Colonial Rule: The Collective Enterprise of Survival*, pp. 286–320, for a nuanced and well-supported discussion of the interchange of superstitions and religious and cosmological belief systems between Europeans and Mayas during the colonial period.

2. This concept has permeated much of the anthropological work on the American Southwest. Unfortunately, the methodology of this approach often rests on descriptions of the elements of the mixture as described by ethnographers observing contemporary Indian-Catholic societies. Few authors have been able to break out of this confine to capture the actual process of syncretism and place it within a proper historical context.

3. France V. Scholes, "Church and State in New Mexico, 1610–1650," *New Mexico Historical Review* 11:1–4 (1936), pp. 9–76, 145–78, 283–94, and 297–349, and 12:1 (January 1937), pp. 78–106 (hereafter cited as "Church and State"); Scholes, *Troublous Times in New Mexico, 1659–1670* (hereafter cited as *Troublous Times*); and Garner, "Seventeenth Century New Mexico." Garner subdivides the community of permanent settlers further, into encomenderos and non-encomenderos, but he fails to develop this differentiation with regard to the overall church-state conflict. A good critique of historiography on the conflict to date

may be found in William H. Broughton, "The History of Seventeenth-Century New Mexico: Is It Time for New Interpretations?" *New Mexico Historical Review* 68:1 (January 1993), pp. 8–10.

4. Scholes, "Church and State," p. 105. Garner rightly points out in his criticisms of Scholes's works that the latter is nothing less than paternalistic in his analysis of the conflict's impact upon Pueblo society. Garner, however, does little to reverse Scholes' interpretation.

Chapter 3

1. George P. Hammond, "Oñate a Marauder?" *New Mexico Historical Review* 10:4 (October 1935), pp. 249–70. Hammond provides translations of documents housed in Guadalajara in which charges were brought against Oñate and his men for plundering the estates of Juan Bautista de Lomas y Colmenares, as well as kidnapping two female Indian servants and a boy from one of those estates. It should be noted, however, that Lomas was one of the two wealthiest landowners on the northern frontier, the other being Oñate. Bautista had himself sought the contract to lead the New Mexico entrada and received an initial go-ahead from Viceroy Villamanrique, only to have that decision overturned by Villamanrique's successor in 1589. Clearly, the potential for personal rivalry between Bautista and Oñate was high, bringing the legitimacy of the charges against Oñate into some question. At the same time, one can think of few potential targets for plunder more tempting to Oñate in his difficulties than the estates of his longtime rival, Bautista.

2. John, *Storms*, p. 56.

3. Valverde Investigation, Herrera Testimony, July 30, 1601, in Hammond and Rey, *Oñate* 2:653.

4. Velasco to the Viceroy, March 22, 1601, *Oñate* 2:210.

5. Proceedings of the Lieutenant Governor with Regard to Breaking Camp, San Gabriel, September 7, 1601, *Oñate* 2:680.

6. Richard B. Woodbury and Ezra B. W. Zubrow, "Agri-

cultural Beginnings, 2000 B.C. to A.D. 500," in *Handbook* 9:43–47 (hereafter cited as "Agricultural Beginnings").

7. Ibid., p. 46.

8. For a detailed discussion of changing weather patterns in the prehistoric Southwest, see Lynn B. Jorde, "Precipitation Cycles and Cultural Buffering in the Southwest," in Lewis Binford, ed., *For Theory Building in Archaeology: Essays on Faunal Remains, Aquatic Resources, Spatial Analysis, and Systemic Modeling*, pp. 385–96. Also see Linda S. Cordell, "Prehistory: Eastern Anasazi," in *Handbook* 9:133–34.

9. Woodbury and Zubrow, "Agricultural Beginnings," *Handbook* 9:52.

10. Valverde Investigation, Herrera Testimony, July 30, 1601, *Oñate* 2:653.

11. Valverde Investigation, Ortega Testimony, July 31, 1601, *Oñate* 2:660.

12. Proceedings of the Lieutenant Governor with Regard to Breaking Camp, San Gabriel, September 7, 1601, *Oñate* 2:684.

13. Valverde Investigation, Herrera Testimony, July 30, 1601, *Oñate* 2:653.

14. Velasco to the Viceroy, March 22, 1601, *Oñate* 2:610.

15. Proceedings of the Lieutenant Governor with Regard to Breaking Camp, San Gabriel, September 7, 1601, *Oñate* 2:680.

16. Velasco to the Viceroy, March 22, 1601, *Oñate* 2:615.

17. Hammond and Rey, *Oñate* 2:609.

18. Desertion of the Colony, Testimony of Captain Bernabe de las Casas, September 7, 1601, *Oñate* 2:687.

19. Velasco to the Viceroy, March 22, 1601, *Oñate* 2:610.

20. Proceedings of the Lieutenant Governor with Regard to Breaking Camp, San Gabriel, September 7, 1601, *Oñate* 2:679.

21. Valverde Investigation, Herrera Testimony, July 30, 1601, *Oñate* 2:653.

22. Hammond and Rey, *Oñate* 2:679–680.

23. Proceedings of the Lieutenant Governor with Regard to Breaking Camp, San Gabriel, September 7, 1601, *Oñate* 2:675.

24. Valverde Inquiry, Rodríguez Testimony, July 30, 1601, *Oñate* 2:870.

25. Fray Escobar's Diary, 1605, *Oñate* 2:1030.

26. Governor Oñate to the Viceroy, August 24, 1607, *Oñate* 2:1044.

27. For much of the following discussion, see John, *Storms*, pp. 55–98, and Albert H. Schroeder, "Shifting for Survival in the Spanish Southwest," *New Mexico Historical Review* 43:4 (October 1968), pp. 291–310 (hereafter cited as "Shifting for Survival").

28. Charles H. Lange, "Relations of the Southwest with the Plains and Great Basin," *Handbook* 10:201–203 (hereafter cited as "Relations").

29. Richard I. Ford, "Inter-Indian Exchange in the Southwest," *Handbook* 10:712.

30. Ibid. 10:711–15.

31. Ibid. 10:711–12.

32. John, *Storms*, p. 62.

33. Hearing of May 11, 1663, Nicolás de Aguilar, in Hackett, *Documents* 3:143.

34. John, *Storms*, p. 55.

35. Lange, "Relations," p. 202; and John, *Storms*, p. 63.

36. John, *Storms*, p. 59.

37. Schroeder, "Shifting for Survival," p. 295; Order Requiring the Governor of New Mexico to Send a Squad of Men to Defend the Spaniards from the Apaches, March 6, 1608, *Oñate* 2:1059; and France V. Scholes, "Juan Martínez de Montoya, Settler and Conquistador of New Mexico," *New Mexico Historical Review* 19:4 (October 1944), p. 340 (hereafter cited as "Martinez").

38. Scholes, "Martinez," p. 340.

39. Order Requiring the Governor of New Mexico to Send a Squad of Men to Defend the Spaniards from the Apaches, March 6, 1608, *Oñate* 2:1059.

40. Don Luis de Velasco to the King, December 17, 1608, *Oñate* 2:1067. Care must be taken in accepting the figure of 7,000 at face value, since the friars may have inflated the numbers to

win continued royal support for their missionary effort. (For a discussion of the difficulties of interpreting baptismal statistics offered by missionaries in newly opened territories, see David Henige, "Native American Population at Contact: Discursive Strategies and Standards of Proof in the Debate," *Latin American Population History Bulletin* 22 (Fall 1992), pp. 2–23.) Still, unless the phenomenon was a complete prevarication on the part of the Franciscans, the report indicates that unprecedented numbers of Pueblos underwent baptism in the spring of 1608.

41. Don Luis de Velasco to the King, December 17, 1608, *Oñate* 2:1080.

42. Memorial of Fray Francisco de Velasco, April 9, 1609, *Oñate* 2:1095.

43. Ibid., p. 1094.

Chapter 4

1. Hearing of June 16, 1663, in Hackett, *Documents* 3:204.

2. See, for instance, France V. Scholes, "Problems in the Early Ecclesiastical History of New Mexico," *New Mexico Historical Review* 7:1 (January 1932), pp. 32–74 (hereafter cited as "Problems").

3. *Fray Alonso de Benavides' Revised Memorial of 1634*, ed. and trans. George P. Hammond, p. 176 (hereafter cited as *Revised Memorial*).

4. Petition of Benavides, January 19, 1635, in Benavides, *Revised Memorial*, p. 66.

5. Governor Peralta's Instructions, March 30, 1609, in Hammond and Rey, *Oñate* 2:1089.

6. Benavides, *Revised Memorial*, p. 69.

7. Valverde Investigation, Horta Testimony, July 30, 1601, *Oñate* 2:648.

8. Benavides, *Revised Memorial*, p. 72.

9. Ibid., p. 214.

10. Ibid., p. 78.

11. Ibid., p. 79.

12. Ibid., p. 70.

13. Ibid., p. 74–75.

14. Memorial of Fray Esteban de Perea, as printed in *Revised Memorial*, p. 214.

15. Benavides, *Revised Memorial*, p. 77.

16. Ibid., p. 78.

17. Ibid., p. 80.

18. See chapter 6; and Spicer, *Cycles of Conquest*, p. 188.

19. Marc Simmons, *New Mexico*, p. 44.

20. Scholes, "Problems," p. 72.

21. Declaration of Isabel Vaca, Santo Domingo, June 18, 1662, in Hackett, *Documents* 3:132.

22. Hearing of February 21, 1661, Mexico, Fray Nicolás de Freitas, *Documents* 3:136.

23. Reply of Mendizabal, *Documents* 3:217.

24. Hearing of February 21, 1661, Mexico, Fray Nicolás de Freitas, *Documents* 3:135.

25. Hall, *Social Change*, p. 89; and Spicer, *Cycles of Conquest*, p. 167, 298.

26. Testimony of Nicolás de Freitas, January 24, 1661, *Documents* 3:163.

27. Benavides, *Revised Memorial*, p. 99.

28. Ibid., p. 59.

29. Ibid., p. 72.

30. The most outrageous of these testimonies was the thirdhand account of Diego García, printed in Scholes, Appendix IV of "The First Decade of the Inquisition in New Mexico," *New Mexico Historical Review* 10:3 (1935), p. 240 (hereafter cited as "Inquisition"): "era verdad que a Pedro de la Cruz lo avian cogido en el Pueblo de San Juan ydolatrando con los indios y que tenia una criatura muerta allí en la estufa, y que yban llegando y ofreciendo al Demonio algodon y otras cosas, y luego llegavan a la criatura y le tiravan con unos frisoles en la vía por donde escrementa, y luego con unas canuelas que llaman Patoles con que juegan los indios tiravan y davan en el petate que estava en el

techo de la estufa y caian sobre el cuerpo de la criatura difunta sin caer ninguna en el suelo, y luego lavaban la criatura con un agua que tenían en un cajete y bebian aquella agua."

31. Declaration of Pedro de la Cruz, September 14, 1632, in Scholes, Appendix IV, "Inquisition," p. 240.

32. For an explanation of the office of fiscal, see Joe Sando, *The Pueblo Indians*, p. 9.

33. See chapter 6.

34. Scholes, *Troublous Times*, p. 69.

35. Hearing of December 19, 1665, *Documents* 3:263.

36. See chapter 8.

37. Hall, *Social Change*, p. 88.

38. See, for instance, Simmons, "History of Pueblo-Spanish Relations to 1821," *Handbook* 9:192–93.

39. See Chapter 7, p. 140; notes 8–13.

40. For a discussion of the interpretation of Inquisition testimony, see Renato Rosaldo, "From the Door of His Tent: The Fieldworker and the Inquisitor," in James Clifford and George Marcus, *Writing Culture: The Poetics and Politics of Ethnography*, pp. 77–97.

41. Declaration of Diego García, March 14, 1632, in Scholes, "Inquisition," p. 240.

42. Ibid.

43. Ibid., p. 241.

44. Declaration of Diego de Santiago, in Scholes, "Inquisition," p. 241.

45. Letter to the Viceroy from the Custodian, November 11, 1659, *Documents* 3:189.

Chapter 5

1. Scholes, "Church and State," p. 155.

2. Ibid., p. 164.

3. Ibid., p. 304.

4. Ibid., p. 311.

5. Ibid., p. 40; Garner, "Seventeenth Century New Mexico," p. 50.

6. The reader should refer especially to the landmark works of France V. Scholes, cited earlier, as well as Garner's cited attempt to critique those works. In his review of the church-state conflict in seventeenth-century New Mexico, Gutiérrez provides an enlightening discussion of the theocratic underpinnings of the Franciscans' perceived charge in the northern territory (see *Corn Mothers*, pp. 65–94).

7. Gutiérrez, *Corn Mothers*, pp. 47–48.

8. Scholes, "Church and State," p. 146.

9. Declaration of Friar Pedro de Ortega, January 27, 1626, in Scholes, "Church and State," p. 166 n. 3.

10. Declaration of Fray Pedro Zambrano, April 20, 1626, ibid., p. 169 n. 15.

11. Declaration of Fray Pedro de Haro de la Cueba, August 22, 1621, ibid., p. 168 n. 10.

12. "Copy of what was provided in an order to the government of New Mexico based on the fifth Chapter of the Government letter of March 10, 1620," ed. and trans. Lansing B. Bloom, in "A Glimpse of New Mexico in 1620," *New Mexico Historical Review* 3:4 (October 1928), p. 368 (hereafter cited as "Orders to Eulate").

13. Scholes, "Church and State," p. 164.

14. Ibid., p. 149. On p. 170 n. 21 and p. 172 n. 41, Scholes refers to an extant copy of such a *vale* signed by Eulate and dated November 15, 1620, in AGN Inquisición 356, ff. 275–6.

15. Declaration of Friar Pedro de Ortega, September 2, 1621, in Scholes, "Church and State," p. 170 n. 17.

16. Bloom, "Orders to Eulate," p. 367.

17. Ibid.

18. Scholes, "Church and State," p. 148; and Declaration of Friar Pedro de Haro, August 22, 1621, ibid., p. 168 n. 13.

19. Ibid., p. 148.

20. Ibid., p. 148; and Declaration of Friar Pedro Zambrano, August 18, 1621, ibid., p. 169 n. 14.

21. Declaration of Friar Pedro Zambrano, August 18, 1621,

ibid., p. 169 n. 14.

22. Ibid.

23. Declaration of Captain Francisco Pérez Granillo, 1626, in Scholes, "Church and State," p. 169 n. 15.

24. Benavides, *Revised Memorial,* p. 71.

25. Scholes, "Church and State," p. 160.

26. As quoted in Scholes, "Church and State," p. 161.

27. See chapter 7.

28. Declaration of Fray Pedro Zambrano, April 20, 1626, in Scholes, "Church and State," p. 172 n. 42. In this case "gentility," by European interpretations of the term, connotes heathenism or paganism.

29. Here again the reader should refer to Scholes, "Church and State," for details of the conflict.

30. See chapter 4.

31. Scholes, "Church and State," p. 288.

32. Rosas's murder occurred shortly after the untimely death of his successor, Juan Flores de Sierra y Valdez. Flores had named his sargento mayor, Francisco Gómez, lieutenant governor shortly before his death, but the newly elected cabildo of Santa Fe (packed, inevitably, with the anti-Rosas elements who had been denied power because of the ex-governor's early machinations) refused to recognize Gómez and, in contradiction to colonial law, declared itself the ruling authority in the province. This provided Rosas's opponents with the opportunity to imprison the ex-governor and engineer his assassination while in custody. Flores's replacement as governor, Alonso de Pacheco y Heredia, arrived in Santa Fe in November 1642. He carried with him the authority to issue a public pardon to all those who had taken part in the events of that year, a move intended to calm the situation sufficiently to allow Pacheco to begin a quiet investigation into the affair. In the event that his investigation revealed the true identity of those behind Rosas's murder and the cabildo's usurpation of power, Pacheco also carried secret instructions "to get rid of them by a brief and exemplary punishment." On July

21, 1643, Pacheco carried out those orders, beheading eight of the province's more prominent soldier-settlers. See Scholes, "Church and State," pp. 297–347, for the detailed narrative of these events, and Garner, "Seventeenth Century New Mexico," p. 49, for a good analysis of the military-clerical alliance that brought Rosas's downfall.

33. Declaration of Fray Antonio de Arteaga, July 14, 1638, in Scholes, "Church and State," p. 328 n. 17.

34. Petition of Salazar, July 5, 1641, ibid., p. 327 n. 9. See also the Declaration of Cristóbal Enríquez, September 11, 1638, and the Declaration of Fray Juan de San Joseph, July 28, 1628, in the same note. Enríquez offered the most detailed depiction of the transaction, claiming that when Rosas attended the yearly trading fair at Pecos, he commanded that the people of Pecos bring him blankets and hides secretly "at night, passing them through a window."

35. Scholes, "Church and State," p. 320, and declarations by Salas (March 16, 1640) and Salazar (July 5, 1641) on p. 332 n. 48.

36. Scholes, *Troublous Times*, p. 19; First Hearing of Don Bernardo López de Mendizabal, in Hackett, *Documents* 3:193; and Accusation of the Fiscal, Don Juan de Ortega Montañez, March 14, 1662, *Documents* 3:186.

37. Letter of the Father Custodian and the *Definidores* of New Mexico to the Viceroy of New Spain, November 11, 1659, *Documents* 3:186.

38. Ibid. 3:188 See Scholes, *Troublous Times*, pp. 47–49, for more detailed listings of López's projects involving Indian laborers.

39. Reply of Mendizabal, *Documents* 3:211.

40. Hearing of June 16, 1663, Requested by López, *Documents* 3:188.

41. Reply of López, *Documents* 3:212.

42. As quoted in Scholes, *Troublous Times*, p. 64.

43. Reply of López, *Documents* 3:213.

44. Scholes, *Troublous Times*, pp. 53–60.

209

45. Ratification by Miguel de Noriega, Santa Fe, September 22, 1661, *Documents* 3:184.

46. Ibid. 3:181.

47. Testimony of Fray Salvador de Guerra, June 13, 1662, *Documents* 3:138.

48. On June 18, 1662, Isabel Vaca, a resident of Tajique, the district seat of Las Salinas, testified that in the winter of 1659–60, Aguilar had forbade "the Indians to carry wood to the convent so that the three religious who were there might warm themselves and cook their food, for so great was the need of those poor fathers that they were burning the crosses used for all the Lenten processions in order to cook a mouthful of food. To this Nicolás de Aguilar replied, laughing: 'Let them burn the crosses, what are the crosses good for except to burn?' . . . His cruelty obliged Fray Juan Ramírez, a religious eighty years old, to go out, falling and trembling with cold, it being Christmas time and the snow deep, to gather a few sticks of wood. Nicolás de Aguilar, seeing this, stood laughing, and was not moved with pity" (Declaration of Isabel Vaca, Santo Domingo, June 18, 1662, *Documents* 3:133). In the mission at Abó, Aguilar reportedly denied Fray Antonio Aguado the services of his Indian translator Bartolomé, threatening Bartolomé with two hundred lashes if he ever entered the convento (Hearing of February 21, 1661, Mexico, Fray Nicolás de Freitas, *Documents* 3:134). And members of the clergy damned López's lieutenant governor as a man "who persecuted them by his writings, prevented them from administering the holy sacrament, took away the cantors, sacristans, and others who attended divine worship, and who beat the Indians in the churches and churchyards to prevent them from serving their spiritual pastors" (Testimony of Fray Salvador de Guerra, June 13, 1662, *Documents* 3:138).

49. Hearing of June 16, 1663, Requested by López, *Documents* 3:209.

50. Copy of a Letter from Fray Miguel de Sacristán, June 16, 1660, *Documents* 3:149.

51. Ibid.

52. Hearing of June 16, 1663, Requested by López, *Documents* 3:200.

53. Reply of López, *Documents* 3:215–16.

54. Hearing of May 11, 1663, *Documents* 3:141.

55. Hearing of June 16, 1663, Requested by López, *Documents* 3:197.

56. Deposition of Nicolás de Aguilar, May 8, 1663, *Documents* 3:169.

57. Reply of López, *Documents* 3:216.

58. Deposition of Nicolás de Aguilar, May 8, 1663, *Documents* 3:170.

59. Ibid.

60. Ibid.; and Hearing of June 16, 1663, Requested by López, *Documents* 3:202.

61. Auto of López, June 12, 1660, *Documents* 3:168.

62. Hearing of February 21, 1661, Mexico, Fray Nicolás de Freitas, *Documents* 3:136.

63. Hearing of June 16, 1663, Requested by López, *Documents* 3:204.

64. Deposition of Nicolás de Aguilar, May 8, 1663, *Documents* 3:173.

65. See, for instance, the Declaration of Captain Diego de Trujillo, Santa Fe, September 22, 1661, *Documents* 3:181.

66. Hearing of February 21, 1661, Mexico, Nicolás de Freitas, *Documents* 3:136.

67. Declaration of Nicolás de Freitas, Mexico, January 10, 1661, *Documents* 3:134; and Testimony of Nicolás de Freitas, January 21, 1661, *Documents* 3:157.

68. Deposition of Thomé Domínquez, Retired Sargento Mayor, Isleta, May 21, 1661, *Documents* 3:179.

69. Reply of Mendizabal, *Documents* 3:223–24.

70. Ibid. 3:222–23.

71. Deposition of Thomé Domínguez, Retired Sargento Mayor, Isleta, May 21, 1661, *Documents* 3:178.

211

72. Testimony of Fray Salvador de Guerra, June 13, 1662, *Documents* 3:138.

73. Deposition of Thomé Domínguez, Retired Sargento Mayor, Isleta, May 21, 1661, *Documents* 3:178.

74. Ibid.

75. Declaration of Fray Benito de la Navidad, Socorro, May 17, 1661, *Documents* 3:184.

76. Letter from Fray Francisco de Salazar, Minister at Senecú, June 17, 1660, *Documents* 3:150.

77. Fray Alonso de Posadas to the Holy Office, May 23, 1661, *Documents* 3:166.

78. Scholes, *Troublous Times*, p. 109. Peñalosa cited a 1648 decree by Governor Guzmán granting each convent ten Pueblo servants exempt from paying tribute.

79. Testimony of Fray Salvador de Guerra, June 13, 1662, *Documents* 3:138.

80. Hearing of June 16, 1663, Requested by López, *Documents* 3:211.

81. Reply of López, *Documents* 3:227.

82. See Scholes, *Troublous Times*, pp. 107–48, 198–244.

Part III

1. Primarily for want of source material, little historical work has been done to date on the fracturing of individual Pueblo communities along economic and sociopolitical lines and the means by which ambitious individuals could use the Spanish colonial system and collaboration with its representatives in New Mexico for personal gain. As noted by authors such as Steve Stern and Nancy Farriss, this dynamic proved common in other Indian communities under Spanish control and severely limited the prospects for any meaningful, long-term resistance to the erosion of their cultural identity in the face of European colonialism. See Steve J. Stern, *Peru's Indian Peoples and the Challenge of Spanish Conquest: Huamanga to 1640* (hereafter cited as *Huamanga*); Nancy M. Farriss, *Maya Society Under Colonial Rule;*

and Inga Clendinnen, *Ambivalent Conquests: Maya and Spaniard in Yucatan, 1517–1570*. On the availability of court records crucial to the understanding of such intracommunity factionalism for New Mexico in the seventeenth century, see Charles R. Cutter, *The Protector de Indios in Colonial New Mexico, 1659–821* (hereafter cited as *Protector de Indios*).

Chapter 6

1. For a more in-depth discussion of much of the following, see W. H. Timmons, *El Paso: A Borderlands History*, pp. 29–31; and Max Moorhead, *New Mexico's Royal Road*, pp. 3–39.

2. "Journey of the dead."

3. In a letter dated December 20, 1680, Fray Francisco de Ayeta described an earlier attempt to lead the wagons under his charge across a flooded Río del Norte: "Being more confident than was justified that I would overcome the dangers and the craftiness of the fierce and irresistible Río del Norte, for its ferocity inspires terror . . . I attached to the leading wagon six files of pack mules, so that the first ones, swimming across to shallow water, might get a footing. In order that the current might not carry away the wagon, I provided for a number of active Indian swimmers, and I got up into the wagon and drove it into the water, invoking the name of God. There we found the danger greater than we had ever thought, for, although God granted that the first mules should gain the islet and do their best to extricate themselves, the water checked my progress, rising more than a vara and a half through the entrance of the wagon. . . . I, clinging to the top, managed quickly to cut loose the files of the mules, that then came out, half drowned. . . . It was not possible to extricate the wagon until, with very great labor, it was accomplished after working from eight in the morning until after six in the evening" (Hackett, *Revolt* 1:212).

4. *Benavides' Memorial of 1630*, trans. Peter P. Forrestal, p. 9 (hereafter cited as *Memorial*).

5. Ibid., p. 10.

6. France V. Scholes, "The Supply Service of the New Mexican Missions in the Seventeenth Century," *New Mexico Historical Review* 5:1 (January 1930), p. 93 (hereafter cited as "Mission Supply").

7. This system functioned on an ad hoc basis in the early decades of the century, but by 1631 a formal contract had been drawn up to cover the details of the arrangement. Only briefly did the crown remove control of the caravan from the Franciscans, contracting instead with private business interests to supply New Mexico's missions from 1664 to 1673. Corruption on the part of those hired by the crown to run the supply convoys forced the viceroy to end the experiment and return effective control of the system to the Franciscans. See Scholes, "Mission Supply," pp. 386–400, and Viceregal Decree Concerning the Contract, ibid., p. 96.)

8. See Patent of the Provincial to Fray Tomás Manso Authorizing Him to Make the Contract, April 13, 1661, in Scholes, "Mission Supply," pp. 99–112.

9. Ibid., p. 98, 186.

10. Ibid., p. 94.

11. Benavides, *Memorial*, p. 12.

12. Ibid.

13. Ibid., pp. 63–65.

14. For an example of the pitfalls of seventeenth-century cartography and navigation, see Peter H. Wood, "La Salle: Discovery of a Lost Explorer," *American Historical Review* 89:2 (April 1984), pp. 294–323 (hereafter cited as "La Salle"). On the Bahía del Espíritu Santo, see Wood, "La Salle," p. 301; and C. J. Lynch in Benavides, *Memorial*, pp. 64–65 nn. 133, 134. For a general discussion of maps and overland navigation in the colonies, see W. P. Cumming et al., *The Exploration of North America, 1630–1776*, pp. 24–25.

15. The Valverde Inspection, Horta Testimony, July 30, 1601, in Hammond and Rey, *Oñate* 2:656.

16. Ibid.

17. Benavides, *Memorial*, p. 41.

18. "Eight months of winter, four months of hell." The Valverde Inspection, Horta Testimony, July 30, 1601, *Oñate* 2:656.

19. Benavides described a hill at Socorro where, in hyperbole typical for the custodian, he claimed that "nowhere in the Indies can silver by more easily extracted" (*Memorial*, p. 17). The Franciscan proceeded to detail how he had obtained samples from a number of veins discovered in that area and at some point had them tested by miners in the camps at Santa Bárbara. The reports having been very positive, Benavides proceeded to theorize as to how the riches might be exploited, noting the proximity of the area to a good water source for mining operations (the Río Grande) and deliberating the pros and cons of subjecting the Pueblos to labor in the mines while attempting to convince them of the benevolence of the Catholic faith. While the custodian's claims are easily dismissed as yet another effort to portray the province in glowing if somewhat exaggerated terms, it is interesting to note that these foothills west of Socorro eventually fueled the spectacular silver boom in New Mexico in the late nineteenth and early twentieth centuries.

20. Discussion and Proposal of the Points Referred to His Majesty Concerning Various Discoveries of New Mexico, *Oñate*, 2:913.

21. Ibid.

22. "A Trade Invoice of 1638 for Goods Shipped by Governor Rosas from Santa Fe," *New Mexico Historical Review* 10:3 (1935), pp. 242–48; and Scholes, "Civil Government and Society," p. 110.

23. Scholes, "Mission Supply," pp. 188–89.

24. Discussion of the Points and Proposal Referred to His Majesty Concerning the Various Discoveries of New Mexico, *Oñate* 2:914.

25. Petition of Fray Francisco de Ayeta, Mexico, May 10, 1679, in Hackett, *Documents* 3:298.

26. New Mexico to be Maintained, January 29, 1609, *Oñate* 2:1077.

27. New Mexico to be Reinforced, March 5, 1609, *Oñate* 2:1082.

28. *Cédula* of His Majesty, Madrid, May 20, 1620, *Documents* 3:47.

29. Marquis of Guadalcazar to the King, May 27, 1620, *Oñate* 2:1140. The term *resident* as used here is somewhat vague. If referring to men, women, and children, it would certainly indicate a decline in population from the sixty settlers listed in 1609. If referring only to those capable of bearing arms, it would still indicate little or no net population growth since Peralta's arrival ten years previously.

30. Benavides, *Revised Memorial*, p. 68. This judgment is based upon Benavides's notorious tendency to inflate his census data for the benefit of royal officials in Mexico City and Spain. His estimate of the Indian population of New Mexico in the late 1620s at half a million is far in excess of the actual number, which measured in the tens of thousands. Also, Benavides records the number of Oñate's original colonists as "seven hundred married Spaniards," when in fact there were only two hundred males, less than a quarter of whom were married.

31. Report to the Viceroy by the Cabildo, February 21, 1639, *Documents* 3:69.

32. Letter of Fray Alonso de Posada, December 4, 1661, as quoted in Scholes, *Troublous Times*, p. 6.

33. Simmons, "History of Pueblo-Spanish Relations to 1821," *Handbook* 9:192.

34. Hackett, for example, takes Otermín's and García's in transit estimates of 1,000 and 1,500 refugees at face value, adds the governor's estimate of 401 casualties in the revolt, and—after acknowledging that some of these numbers included Indian servants—arrives at a figure of 2,800 for New Mexico's Hispanic population in early 1680. Hackett disregards the discrepancy between the 1,946 persons counted in the muster by reasoning that the difference between the 2,500 estimate and the count at

La Salineta simply indicates that the number of refugees who evaded the muster by crossing into Nueva Vizcaya was "at least several hundred" (see Hackett, *Documents* 3:327–28 n. 133, and *Revolt*, p. cix.) Espinosa agrees with this estimate; see José Manuel Espinosa, *Crusaders of the Rio Grande: The Story of Don Diego de Vargas and the Reconquest of New Mexico*, pp. 16, 19 (hereafter cited as *Crusaders of the Rio Grande*).

Scholes, on the other hand, disregards the number of refugees who fled to Nueva Vizcaya before the muster, and adds the 1946 counted at La Salineta to the estimate of 401 casualties from the revolt to reach a total of 2,347 persons, including servants. Although he is somewhat more liberal than Hackett in estimating the number of persons of non-European descent included in this figure, Scholes offsets this consideration with an estimate of the Hispanics killed in Apache raids and famine in the decade and a half prior to 1680, who numbered in the hundreds. As a result, his estimate for the prerevolt Hispanic population stands at 2,300–2,400 (see Scholes, "Civil Government and Society," p. 96.)

These early estimates have resurfaced time and again in the works of more recent historians (see, for example, Simmons, "History of Pueblo-Spanish Relations to 1821," in *Handbook* 9:186, and Garner, "Seventeenth Century New Mexico," p. 61).

35. See chapter 7.

36. Auto for Passing Muster, Reviewing Arms and Horses, and Other Things, La Salineta, September 29 and October 2, 1680, *Revolt* 1:134–53, 156–59.

37. Ayeta to the Viceroy, El Paso, September 16, 1680, *Revolt* 1:126.

38. Record and List of Payments Made to Settlers, El Paso, September 22–October 16, 1681, *Revolt* 2:94–134; and Scholes, "Civil Government and Society," p. 100.

Chapter 7

1. The Muster Roll, January 8, 1598, in Hammond and Rey, *Oñate* 1:289.

2. Manifest of Don Luis de Velasco, in Hackett, *Documents* 1:429–33.

3. First Hearing of Nicolás de Aguilar, Mexico, April 12, 1663, *Documents* 3:139.

4. Ibid.

5. Valverde Inspection, Espinosa Testimony, July 28, 1601, *Oñate* 2:638.

6. Fray Esteban de Perea, January 27, 1632, *Inquisición, Tom. 372*, AGN (Scholes transcript, Box 4615).

7. As quoted in Scholes, *Troublous Times*, p. 228.

8. Ibid., p. 223.

9. Ibid., p. 308.

10. Ibid., p. 7; and Fray Juan Bernal to the Tribunal, April, 1, 1669, *Documents* 3:270.

11. Ibid., p. 7; and Hearing of December 10, 1665, *Documents*, 3:265.

12. Scholes, *Troublous Times*, p. 7; Fray Juan Bernal to the Tribunal, April 1, 1669, *Documents* 3:270; and Declaration of Joseph Nieto, January 19, 1667, *Documents* 3:272.

13. Scholes, *Troublous Times*, p. 7; and Letter from the Governor and Captain General, Don Antonio de Otermín, September 8, 1680, *Documents* 3:334.

14. Reply of Mendizabal, *Documents* 3:217.

15. Fray Alonso de Posadas to the Holy Office, May 23, 1662, *Documents* 3:149.

16. Deposition of Nicolás de Aguilar, May 8, 1663, *Documents* 3:171.

17. Ibid.

18. See chapter 5.

19. Benavides, *Revised Memorial*, p. 98.

20. The Valverde Investigation, Horta Testimony, July 30, 1601, in Hammond and Rey, *Oñate* 2:655.

21. Fray Estevan de Perea, November 10, 1631, *Inquisición, Tom. 372*, AGN (Scholes transcripts, Box 4615).

22. The 1631 contract for the supply of the New Mexico

missions listed some provisions under the specific title of "For the Infirmary" (see Viceregal Decree Concerning the Contract, April 13, 1631, in Scholes, "Mission Supply," p. 101). Hints that this infirmary was located in the mission at San Felipe surface in a 1744 description of that pueblo: "Prior to the uprising of the year 1680 [the convent] was situated on the summit of a hill. . . . This convent, at the time of its erection, was the general hospital of the *custodia*, where the missionary religious and other persons were treated when they were ill" (Declaration of Fray Miguel de Menchero, Santa Bárbara, May 10, 1744, in *Documents* 3:394).

23. Of the 81,000 pesos spent in Mexico City to outfit the supply train bound for the northern missions in 1629, 1,200 went to the acquisition of various drugs and medicinal preserves. See Lansing B. Bloom, "Fray Estevan de Perea's *Relación*," *New Mexico Historical Review* 8:3 (July 1933), p. 220.

24. Viceregal Decree Concerning the Contract, April 13, 1631, in Scholes, "Mission Supply," p. 101.

25. Testimony of Petronilla de Zamora, March 25, 1631, *Inquisición, Tom. 372*, AGN (Scholes Transcript, Box 4615): "havia oido desir esta declarante que [de los Angeles] era echisera de compacion . . . "

26. Testimony of Catalina Bernal, March 25, 1631, *Inquisición, Tom. 372*, AGN (Scholes transcripts, Box 4615).

27. See, for instance, the testimonies of Ana Cadimo (March 25, 1631), Juana Sánchez (June 22, 1631), and Catalina Bernal (March 26, 1631), *Inquisición, Tom. 372*, AGN (Scholes transcript, Box 4615). Sánchez testified that de los Angeles had given her the prescription as early as 1620, while others admitted to following the mestiza's advice in the later part of the decade.

28. Testimony of Catalina de Bustillos, March 26, 1631, *Inquisición, Tom. 372*, AGN (Scholes transcript, Box 4615).

29. Testimony of Ana Cadimo, March 25, 1631, *Inquisición, Tom. 372*, AGN (Scholes transcript, Box 4615): "Ana Cadimo . . . dice y denuncia . . . q un año poco mas o menos q diciendile los indios . . . que estaba enechisada y q tomase el peiote i con el

veria a quien le avia enechisado y hecho mal, q viendolo sanaria
luego y veria tambien el echiso y donde estaba y . . . q buscase un
indio q se lo diese y asi busco un indio biejo de san marcos de
nacion qres el qual tomo lio i dio vever con un poco de agua a esta
declarante. . . . Dice mas esta declarante q abra dos o tres años q
una india tegua del pueblo de S. ildefonso llamada francisca
latiphaña le dio a vever otras ierbas desechas en un jumate de
agua . . . pero primero que la india se lo diese a vever asia algunas
seremonias i conjuros y contaba y . . . q via en algunos visiones
en el agua . . . y asia la musica y ablaba. . . . No sabe otra cosa mas
de q agora dos años esta mesma india . . . se desia publicamente
en esta villa q avia tomado el peiote para ver quien venia de tierra
de pas."

30. Testimony of Juana de los Reyes, June 21, 1631, *Inquisición, Tom. 372*, AGN (Scholes transcript, Box 4615).

31. Testimony of Juana Sánchez, June 22, 1631, *Inquisición,
Tom. 372*, AGN (Scholes Transcript, Box 4615).

32. Denunciation by María de Abisu, Santa Fe, November 4,
1661, in Hackett, *Documents* 3:183.

33. Testimony of Nicolás de Freitas, January 25, 1661, *Documents* 3:161. See also John L. Kessell, "Diego Romero, the Plains
Apaches, and the Inquisition," *The American West* 15 (May–June
1978), pp. 12–16.

34. Fray Esteban de Perea, November 10, 1631, *Inquisición,
Tom. 372*, AGN (Scholes transcript, Box 4615).

Chapter 8

1. Simmons, "History of Pueblo-Spanish Relations to
1821," *Handbook* 9:192.

2. For a good example of the usefulness of this type of
evidence in reconstructing a portion of New Mexico's epidemic
history, see Marc Simmons, "New Mexico's Smallpox Epidemic
of 1780–1781," *New Mexico Historical Review* 41:4 (October 1966),
pp. 319–26.

3. See chapter 3.

4. For a discussion of this phenomenon, see Woodrow Borah and S. F. Cook, "The Population of the Yucatán," in *Essays in Population History: Mexico and the Caribbean*, 3 vols.; and Henry F. Dobyns, *Their Number Become Thinned: Native American Population Dynamics in Eastern North America*, p. 12 (hereafter cited as *Their Number Become Thinned*).

5. Dobyns, *Their Number Become Thinned*, pp. 13, 15.

6. Cabeza de Vaca, *Relación*, pp. 113–14.

7. Hall, *Social Change*, p. 76; and John, *Storms*, p. 87.

8. Brief and True Account of the Discovery of New Mexico by Nine Men Who Set Out From Santa Bárbara in the Company of Three Franciscan Friars, in Hammond and Rey, *Rediscovery*, p. 142. On the advisability of taking such firsthand estimates at face value, see Borah and Cook, "Materials for the Demographic History of Mexico," in *Essays in Population History: Mexico and the Caribbean* 1:7–14.

9. Petition of Father Juan de Prada, Mexico, September 26, 1638, in Hackett, *Documents* 3:108.

10. Declaration of Fray Juan Alvarez, Nambé, January 12, 1706, *Documents* 3:372–78.

11. Petition of Fray Juan de Prada, Mexico, September 26, 1638, *Documents* 3:108.

12. "Petition of Fray Francisco de Ayeta, Mexico, May 10, 1679," *Documents* 3:299. For a more detailed listing of Pueblo population estimates for the entire colonial period, see Simmons, "The History of Pueblo-Spanish Relations to 1821," *Handbook* 9:185.

13. Petition of Fray Juan de Prada, Mexico, September 26, 1638, *Documents* 3:108. Debate continues on the true nature and identity of the microorganism responsible for cocolitzli, a Nahua term denoting nothing more specific than "sickness." Nevertheless, some researchers have argued that the symptomatological descriptions that at times accompany documentary references to the disease are consistent with a variation of pneumonic plague. See Elsa Malvido and Carlos Viesca, "La

epidemia de cocoliztli de 1576," *Historias* 1 (1985), pp. 27–34.

14. Scholes, "Church and State," p. 324.

15. Petition of Fray Francisco de Ayeta, Mexico, May 10, 1679, *Documents* 3:302.

16. See chapter 3.

17. Hearing of June 16, 1663, Requested by Mendizábal, *Documents* 3:204.

18. Gutiérrez, *Corn Mothers*, p. 117; and Petition of Fray Juan de Prada, Mexico, September 26, 1638, *Documents* 3:110.

19. Fray Juan Bernal to the Tribunal, April 1, 1669, from the convent of Santo Domingo, *Documents* 3:272.

20. Petition of Fray Francisco de Ayeta, Mexico, May 10, 1679, *Documents* 3:302.

21. See note 15, this chapter, for Fray Francisco de Ayeta's reference to the 1671 epidemic.

22. Letter of the Father Custodian and the *Definidores* to the Viceroy of New Spain, November 11, 1659, *Documents* 3:186.

23. Ibid.

24. Ibid.

25. Hall, *Social Change*, p. 84; and Garner, "Seventeenth Century New Mexico," p. 52.

26. Scholes, "Church and State," p. 324; Forbes, *Apache, Navajo, and Spaniard*, pp. 150–51; Simmons, "History of Pueblo-Spanish Relations to 1821," p. 184; and Gutiérrez, *Corn Mothers*, p. 112.

27. Fray Juan Bernal to the Tribunal, April 1, 1669, from the convent of Santo Domingo, *Documents* 3:272.

28. Petition of Fray Francisco de Ayeta, Mexico, May 10, 1679, *Documents* 3:299.

29. Ibid.

30. Forbes, *Apache, Navajo, and Spaniard*, pp. 150–51; and Simmons, "History of Pueblo-Spanish Relations to 1821," p. 184.

31. Petition of Fray Francisco de Ayeta, Mexico, May 10, 1679, *Documents* 3:297.

32. Ibid. 3:298.

33. Albert H. Schroeder, "Pueblos Abandoned in Historic Times," *Handbook* 9:241.

34. Petition of Fray Francisco de Ayeta, Mexico, May 10, 1679, *Documents* 3:297.

35. Declaration of the Indian Juan, December 18, 1681, in Hackett, *Revolt* 2:245.

36. Declaration of Diego López Sambrano, December 22, 1681, *Revolt* 2:300–301.

37. Declaration of the Lt. General of the Cavalry, December 20, 1681, *Revolt* 2:226.

38. Declaration of Pedro Naranjo of the Queres Nation, San Felipe, December 19, 1681, *Revolt* 2:245.

39. See John L. Kessell, "Esteban Clemente, Precursor of the Pueblo Revolt," *El Palacio* 86:4 (1980), pp. 16–17.

40. Declaration of Diego López Sambrano, December 22, 1681, *Revolt* 2:300.

41. Ibid.

42. Letter from Fray Antonio de Sierra to the Father *Visitador*, September 4, 1680, *Revolt* 1:59.

43. Declaration of Diego López Sambrano, December 22, 1681, *Revolt* 2:300; and Jane C. Sánchez, "Spanish-Indian Relations during the Otermín Administration, 1677–1683," *New Mexico Historical Review* 58:2 (1983), pp. 139–40 (hereafter cited as "Spanish-Indian Relations").

44. Declaration of Pedro Naranjo of the Queres Nation, San Felipe, December 19, 1681, *Revolt* 2:246.

45. Ibid.

46. Ibid., p. 248. Fray Angelico Chávez has hypothesized that, unbeknownst to the Spaniards conducting this interrogation, it was in fact either Naranjo himself or a brother named Domingo who planned and led the 1680 revolt, not Popé. Chávez therefore argues that this account of the planning phase of the rebellion was false, a smokescreen thrown out by Naranjo to obscure the true identity of the leader of the movement. To support his views, the author notes the inconsistency of a Keres

Indian referring to Lake Copala in central Mexico, a location with no meaning in Pueblo mythology. Chávez likewise considers the names Caudi, Tilini, and Theume to be derivatives of names of Nahua deities, with no basis in Pueblo cosmology. See Fray Angelico Chávez, "Pohé-Yemo's Representative and the Pueblo Revolt of 1680," *New Mexico Historical Review* 62:2 (April 1967), p. 101, 120 n. 35 (hereafter cited as "Pohé-Yemo").

47. Hackett, *Revolt*, 2:246; Sando, *The Pueblo Indians*, p. 55; Sando, "The Pueblo Revolt," *Handbook* 9:195; Gutiérrez, *Corn Mothers*, p. 132; and Chávez, "Pohé-Yemo," p. 86.

48. Sando, "The Pueblo Revolt," *Handbook* 9:195; and Gutiérrez, *Corn Mothers*, p. 132.

49. Declaration of the Indian Juan, December 18, 1681, *Revolt* 2:234–35.

50. Ibid.

51. Declaration of Pedro Naranjo of the Queres Nation, December 19, 1681, *Revolt* 2:246.

52. Declaration of the Indian Juan, December 18, 1681, *Revolt* 2:234–35.

53. Autos Drawn Up as a Result of the Rebellion of the Christian Indians, Santa Fe, August 9, 1681, *Revolt* 1:3. Pueblo historian Joe S. Sando speculates that the two messengers were probably arrested in either San Cristóbal or Galisteo while en route from Tesuque to Pecos.

54. Hackett, *Revolt* 1:3–5; and Sando, "The Pueblo Revolt," in *Handbook* 9:196.

Epilogue

1. Opinion of the Cabildo of Santa Fe, La Salineta, October 4, 1680, in Hackett, *Revolt* 2:180.

2. Order of the Governor and Captain-General of El Parral, September 24, 1680, *Revolt* 1:184.

3. Reply of the Fiscal, Mexico, January 7, 1681, *Revolt* 1:233.

4. *Revolt* 1:cxxi–cxxiv.

5. For a detailed narrative of the expedition's actions and

movements, see Hackett's introduction to *Revolt* 1:cxx–ccx; and John, *Storms*, pp. 107–10. For a dissection of the internal tensions within the Hispanic expedition and subsequent effects on the treatment of Pueblo prisoners taken during the entrada, see Sánchez, "Spanish-Indian Relations," pp. 137–41.

6. As quoted in Sánchez, "Spanish-Indian Relations," p. 139.

7. John, *Storms*, p. 105; Declaration of Jerónimo, A Tiwa Indian, January 1, 1682, *Revolt* 2:361; and Reply of the Fiscal, Mexico, June 25, 1682, *Revolt* 2:382.

8. See chapter 8.

9. Declaration of One of the Rebellious Christian Indians Who Was Captured on the Road, El Alamillo, September 6, 1680, *Revolt* 1:61.

10. Declaration of the Indian Juan, December 18, 1681, *Revolt* 2:235.

11. Sánchez, "Pueblo-Indian Relations," p. 138; and Espinosa, *Crusaders of the Rio Grande*, pp. 22–23.

12. Sánchez, "Pueblo-Indian Relations," p. 138; Espinosa, *Crusaders of the Rio Grande*, pp. 22–23; Reply of the Fiscal, Mexico, June 25, 1682, *Revolt* 2:382.

13. Sánchez, "Spanish-Indian Relations," p. 145.

14. This is based on the testimony of Juan Punssili, a Picurís native interrogated in El Paso on July 30, 1683. See Sánchez, "Spanish-Indian Relations," pp. 144–45.

15. Ibid., pp. 144–47; and John L. Kessell and Rick Hendricks, eds., *By Force of Arms: The Journals of Don Diego de Vargas, New Mexico, 1691–1693*, pp. 20–22 (hereafter cited as *By Force of Arms*).

16. Many resettled in Nueva Vizcaya, Sonora, and Sinoloa. When Diego de Vargas launched his successful campaign to retake northern New Mexico, few of these refugees answered the governor's and the viceroy's orders to join the expedition, and in fact only a small number of those former colonists who remained in El Paso took part in the entrada. See Espinosa, *Crusaders of the*

Rio Grande, p. 44; and John L. Kessell, "Spaniards and Pueblos: From Crusading Intolerance to Pragmatic Accommodation," in David Hurst Thomas, ed., *Columbian Consequences, Volume I: Archaeological and Historical Perspectives on the Spanish Borderlands West*, p. 134 (hereafter cited as "Spaniards and Pueblos").

17. For a good summary of English machinations in this region in the closing decades of the seventeenth century, see Weber, *Spanish Frontier*, pp. 141–45. See also pp. 147–203 for a good overview of European rivalries on the continent in the late seventeenth and early eighteenth centuries.

18. Spanish perceptions of and reactions to the French incursion are discussed in John, *Storms*, p. 112; Weber, *Spanish Frontier*, pp. 147–52; and Wood, "La Salle."

19. For this violent chapter in the history of New Spain, see especially Forbes, *Apache, Navajo, and Spaniard*; Oakah Jones, *Nueva Vizcaya: Heartland of the Spanish Frontier*; the documentary materials provided in Thomas H. Naylor and Charles W. Polzer, *The Presidio and Militia on the Northern Frontier of New Spain, 1570–1700*, pp. 483–718 (hereafter cited as *Presidio and Militia*); and Maria Elena Galaviz de Capdevielle, *Rebeliones indígenas en el norte del reino de la Nueva España (siglos XVI y XVII)*, pp. 133–40.

20. Real Cédula, Madrid, September 4, 1683, in Kessel and Hendricks, *By Force of Arms*, p. 157. The 1689 cédula appears in *By Force of Arms*, pp. 163–64. See also Meeting of the Finance Committee, May 28, 1692, translated versions of which appear in J. Manuel Espinosa, ed. and trans., *First Expedition of Vargas into New Mexico, 1692*, pp. 43–47 (hereafter cited as *First Expedition*) and *By Force of Arms*, pp. 196–99. Further discussion of the difficulties that the treasury faced in financing a New Mexico expedition in these years appears in Espinosa, *Crusaders of the Rio Grande*, p. 45. As Diego de Vargas prepared to launch his expedition to retake New Mexico during the summer of 1691, treasury officials supported the decision to divert his forces to take part in a joint campaign against Indian insurgents to the

west, which combined forces from Sinaloa, Sonora, and El Paso. In their opinion of August 3, 1691, the officials noted that up until the present there had been no "definite reason compelling the entrada the governor of New Mexico intends to make to the villa of Santa Fe," and declared that after the completion of the western campaign "it will be decided whether it is advantageous to carry out the entradas which he intends to make to the villa of Santa Fe." At the same time, they emphasized that should the expedition be approved, "attention will be paid to the expenses the royal treasury may incur, because of the high costs already occasioned in the wars of the conspiracies in New Biscay and Sinoloa" (Junta of the Treasury, August 3, 1991, in *By Force of Arms*, p. 72).

21. J. Manuel Espinosa, ed. and trans., *The Pueblo Indian Revolt of 1696 and the Franciscan Missions in New Mexico: Letters of the Missionaries and Related Documents*, p. 37 (hereafter cited as *Revolt of 1696*); and Kessell and Hendricks, *By Force of Arms*, p. 22–25. For documentary examples of the participation of the El Paso *presidio* in these campaigns, see Naylor and Polzer, *Presidio and Militia*, pp. 506–47.

22. Espinosa, *Revolt of 1696*, p. 37; and Kessell and Hendricks, *By Force of Arms*, pp. 24–26. Reneros reached as far north as the pueblo of Zía in 1688 and raided Santa Ana while en route. Little documentary evidence of the expedition has been uncovered. Jironza headed north with 80 Spaniards and 120 Indian auxiliaries on August 10, 1689, the ninth anniversary of the Spanish defeat by the Pueblos. Arriving at Zía in late August, the governor launched a full-scale attack on the defiant inhabitants of the pueblo, burning the village to the ground and, by some reports, killing as many as 600 of its defenders. The governor then publicly executed four of the pueblo's leaders before returning south to El Paso with 70 prisoners taken during the encounter.

23. For a comprehensive historical analysis of Vargas's reconquest of New Mexico, the reader should refer to Espinosa,

Crusaders of the Rio Grande, as well as the introductory passages and documentary material presented in Espinosa, *First Expedition;* Kessell and Hendricks, *By Force of Arms;* and John L. Kessell et al., eds. and trans., *Remote Beyond Compare: Letters of Don Diego de Vargas to His Family from New Spain and New Mexico, 1675–1706.* The ensuing paragraphs are based upon these works.

24. The very interesting *petición* by de la Huerta may be found in *By Force of Arms,* pp. 159–61.

25. For Vargas's political connections and machinations within official circles in Mexico City and Madrid, see Kessell and Hendricks, *By Force of Arms,* pp. 30–37.

26. Espinosa, *Revolt of 1696,* p. 38; and Kessell and Hendricks, *By Force of Arms,* pp. 26–27.

27. See, for instance, John L. Kessell, *Kiva, Cross, and Crown: The Pecos Indians and New Mexico, 1540–1840,* pp. 246–53, for Vargas's careful and successful handling of internal dissention within the Pecos community.

28. See Espinosa, *Crusaders of the Rio Grande,* pp. 134–35, for indecision on the part of the inhabitants of Zia.

29. Myra Ellen Jenkins, "Spanish Land Grants in the Tewa Area," *New Mexico Historical Review* 47:2 (April 1972), p. 117 (hereafter cited as "Spanish Land Grants").

30. A full discussion of the 1696 revolt, with rich documentary material surrounding the event, may be found in Espinosa, *Revolt of 1696.*

31. Letter of Fray Francisco de Vargas to the Commissary General, Santa Fe, July 21, 1696, in Espinosa, *Revolt of 1696,* p. 245.

32. Espinosa, *Revolt of 1696,* p. 55; and Joe S. Sando, *Pueblo Nations: Eight Centuries of Pueblo Indian History,* pp. 38, 75.

33. For a concise overview of colonial New Mexican history as a breakdown into pre-revolt, revolt and reconquest, and post-reconquest phases, see Kessell, "Spaniards and Pueblos."

34. Oakah L. Jones, *Pueblo Warriors and Spanish Conquest,* remains the definitive work on this aspect of Pueblo-Spanish cooperation throughout the eighteenth century.

35. Kessell, "Spaniards and Pueblos," p. 132.

36. Ibid., pp. 128, 132; Espinosa, *Crusaders of the Rio Grande*, pp. 363–71; and Weber, *Spanish Frontier*, pp. 212–13. Kessell argues that as the Franciscans reestablished themselves in New Mexico in the decades after the reconquest, their missionary efforts moved "from self-assured intolerance to despairing accommodation" (p. 128).

37. Gutiérrez, *Corn Mothers*, pp. 298–315; and Cutter, *Protector de Indios*, pp. 41–80. For a discussion of the almost century-long legislative battle by the inhabitants of San Ildefonso to protect their village lands, see Jenkins, "Spanish Land Grants," pp. 120–29.

38. Kessell, "Spaniards and Pueblos," p. 134; and Gutiérrez, *Corn Mothers*, p. 173.

39. Alicia V. Tjarks, "Demographic, Ethnic, and Occupational Structure of New Mexico, 1790," *The Americas* 35 (1978–79), p. 82 (hereafter cited as "Occupational Structure").

40. A detailed quantitative analysis of endogamy and exogamy rates among the peoples of New Mexico in the eighteenth century may be found in Tjarks, "Occupational Structure," pp. 72–76 and 78–82.

41. Cutter, *Protector de Indios*, p. 79. A similar dynamic in Native American societies under Spanish colonial rule is explained by Stern in *Huamanga* and Farriss in *Maya Society Under Colonial Rule*. See note 1 to the introduction to part III.

42. Kessell, "Spaniards and Pueblos," p. 128; and Spicer, *Cycles of Conquest*, pp. 502–38.

Works Cited

Primary Sources

Benavides, Fray Alonso de. *Memorial of 1630.* Translated by Peter P. Forrestal. Washington, D.C.: Academy of American Franciscan History, 1954.

———. *Fray Alonso de Benavides' Revised Memorial of 1634.* Edited and translated by George P. Hammond. Albuquerque: University of New Mexico Press, 1945.

Bloom, Lansing B., ed. and trans. "Copy of what was provided in an order to the government of New Mexico based on the fifth Chapter of the Government letter of March 10, 1620." In "A Glimpse of New Mexico in 1620." *New Mexico Historical Review* 3:4 (October 1928), pp. 357–89.

———. "The Royal Order of 1620 to Custodian Fray Esteban de Perea." *New Mexico Historical Review* 5:3 (July 1930), pp. 288–98.

———. "A Trade Invoice for 1638 for Goods Shipped by Governor Rosas from Santa Fe." *New Mexico Historical Review* 10:3 (July 1935), pp. 242–48.

Colección de documentos inéditos relativos al descubrimiento, conquista, y organización de las antiguas posesiones de América y Oceania. Volume 16. Madrid, 1871.

Espinosa, José Manuel, ed. and trans. *First Expedition of Vargas into New Mexico, 1692.* Albuquerque: University of New Mexico Press, 1940.

———. *The Pueblo Indian Revolt of 1696 and the Franciscan Missions in New Mexico: Letters of the Missionaries and Related Documents.* Norman: University of Oklahoma Press, 1988.

Favata, Martín A., and José B. Fernández, eds. *La relación o naufragios de Alvar Núñez Cabeza de Vaca* (1542). Potomac, Md.: Scripta Humanistica, 1986.

Hackett, Charles Wilson, ed. *Historical Documents Relating to New Mexico, Nueva Vizcaya, and Approaches Thereto, to 1773.* Translated by Adolph F. A. and Fanny R. Bandelier. 3 vols. Washington, D.C.: Carnegie Institution, 1937.

———. *Revolt of the Pueblo Indians of New Mexico and Otermín's Attempted Reconquest, 1680–1682.* Translated by Charmion C. Shelby. 2 vols. Albuquerque: University of New Mexico Press, 1942.

Hammond, George P., ed. and trans. *Narratives of the Coronado Expedition, 1540–1542.* Albuquerque: University of New Mexico Press, 1949.

Hammond, George P., and Agapito Rey, eds. and trans. *Expedition into New Mexico Made by Antonio de Espejo, 1582–1583, As Revealed in the Journal of Diego Pérez de Luxán, a Member of the Party.* Los Angeles: Quivira Society Publications, 1929.

———. *Don Juan de Oñate, Colonizer of New Mexico, 1595–1628.* 2 vols. Albuquerque: University of New Mexico Press, 1953.

————. *The Rediscovery of New Mexico, 1580–1594: The Explorations of Chamuscado, Espejo, Castaño de Sosa, Morlete, and Leyva de Bonilla and Humaña*. Albuquerque: University of New Mexico Press, 1966.

Kessell, John L., and Rick Hendricks, eds. and trans. *By Force of Arms: The Journals of Don Diego de Vargas, New Mexico, 1691–1693*. Albuquerque: University of New Mexico Press, 1992.

Kessell, John L., Rick Hendricks, Meredith D. Dodge, and Eleanor B. Adams, eds. and trans. *Remote Beyond Compare: Letters of Don Diego de Vargas to His Family from New Spain and New Mexico, 1675–1706*. Albuquerque: University of New Mexico Press, 1989.

Naylor, Thomas H., and Charles W. Polzer, eds. *The Presidio and Militia on the Northern Frontier of Spain, 1570–1700*. Tucson: University of Arizona Press, 1986.

Pérez de Villagrá, Gaspar. *History of New Mexico* (1610). Translated by Gilberto Espinosa. Los Angeles: Quivira Society Publications, 1933.

Scholes, France V. Transcripts of documents housed in the Archivo General de la Nación Mexicana, Sección de la Inquisición. Library of Congress, Manuscript Division, Washington, D.C.

Turanzas, José Porrua, ed. *Documentos para servir a la historia de Nuevo México, 1583–1778*. Madrid, 1962.

Secondary Sources

Bannon, John F. *Bolton and the Spanish Borderlands*. Norman: University of Oklahoma Press, 1964.

Bloom, Lansing B. "Fray Estévan de Perea's *Relación*." *New Mexico Historical Review* 8:3 (July 1933), pp. 211–35.

Bolton, Herbert E. *Coronado on the Turquoise Trail: Knight of Pueblos and Plains*. Albuquerque: University of New Mexico Press, 1949.

Borah, Woodrow, and S. F. Cook. *Essays in Population History:*

Mexico and the Caribbean. 3 vols. Berkeley: University of California Press, 1971, 1974, 1979.

Broughton, William H. "The History of Seventeenth-Century New Mexico: Is It Time for New Interpretations?" *New Mexico Historical Review* 68:1 (January 1993), pp. 3–12.

Chávez, Fray Angélico. "Pohé-Yemo's Representative and the Pueblo Revolt of 1680." *New Mexico Historical Review* 62:2 (April 1967), pp. 85–126.

Clendinnen, Inga. *Ambivalent Conquests: Maya and Spaniard in Yucatán, 1517–1570.* Cambridge: Cambridge University Press, 1987.

Clifford, James, and George E. Marcus. *Writing Culture: The Poetics and Politics of Ethnography.* Berkeley: University of California Press, 1986.

Coles, Robert. *The Call of Stories: Teaching and the Moral Imagination.* Boston: Houghton Mifflin, 1989.

Cordell, Linda S. "Prehistory: Eastern Anasazi." In *Handbook of North American Indians, Volume 9: The Southwest,* edited by Alfonso Ortíz, pp. 131–51. Washington, D.C.: Smithsonian Institution, 1979.

Cumming, W. P., S. E. Hillier, D. B. Quinn, and G. Williams. *The Exploration of North America, 1630–1776.* New York: G. P. Putnam's Sons, 1974.

Cutter, Charles R. *The Protector de Indios in Colonial New Mexico, 1659–1821.* Albuquerque: University of New Mexico Press, 1986.

Dobyns, Henry F. *Their Number Become Thinned: Native American Population Dynamics in Eastern North America.* Knoxville: University of Tennessee Press, 1983.

Dozier, Edward P. "The Pueblo Indians of the Southwest." *Current Anthropology* 5:2 (April 1964), pp. 79–97.

Espinosa, José Manuel. *Crusaders of the Rio Grande: The Story of Don Diego de Vargas and the Reconquest of New Mexico.* Chicago: Institute of Jesuit History, 1942.

Farriss, Nancy M. *Maya Society Under Colonial Rule: The Collective Enterprise of Survival.* Princeton, N.J.: Princeton University Press, 1984.

Forbes, Jack. *Apache, Navajo, and Spaniard.* Norman: University of Oklahoma Press, 1960.

Ford, Richard I. "Inter-Indian Exchange in the Southwest." In *Handbook of North American Indians, Volume 9: The Southwest,* edited by Alfonso Ortíz, pp. 711–21. Washington, D.C.: Smithsonian Institution, 1979.

Galaviz de Capdevielle, Maria Elena. *Rebeliones indígenas en el norte del reino de la Nueva España (siglos XVI y XVII).* Mexico, D.F.: Editorial Campesina, 1967.

García-Mason, Velma. "Acoma Pueblo." In *Handbook of North American Indians, Volume 9: The Southwest,* edited by Alfonso Ortíz, pp. 450–66. Washington, D.C.: Smithsonian Institution, 1979.

Garner, Van Hastings. "Seventeenth Century New Mexico." *Journal of Mexican-American Studies* 4 (1974), pp. 41–70.

Gutiérrez, Ramón A. *When Jesus Came the Corn Mothers Went Away: Marriage, Sexuality, and Power in New Mexico, 1500–1846.* Stanford, Calif.: Stanford University Press, 1991.

Hall, Thomas D. *Social Change in the Southwest, 1350–1880.* Lawrence: University of Kansas Press, 1989.

Hammond, George P. "Oñate a Marauder?" *New Mexico Historical Review* 10:4 (October 1935), pp. 249–70.

Henige, David. "Native American Population at Contact: Discursive Strategies and Standards of Proof in the Debate." *Latin American Population History Bulletin* 22 (Fall 1992), pp. 2–23.

Jenkins, Myra Ellen. "Spanish Land Grants in the Tewa Area." *New Mexico Historical Review* 47:2 (April 1972), pp. 113–34.

John, Elizabeth A. H. *Storms Brewed in Other Men's Worlds: The Confrontation of Indians, Spanish, and French in the*

Works Cited

Southwest, 1540–1795. College Station: Texas A & M University Press, 1975.

———. "A View from the Spanish Borderlands." In *Proceedings of the American Antiquarian Society* 1:101 (1991), pp. 77–87.

Jones, Oakah L. *Pueblo Warriors and Spanish Conquest.* Norman: University of Oklahoma Press, 1966.

———. *Nueva Vizcaya: Heartland of the Spanish Frontier.* Albuquerque: University of New Mexico Press, 1988.

Jorde, Lynn B. "Precipitation Cycles and Cultural Buffering in the Southwest." In *For Theory Building in Archaeology: Essays on Faunal Remains, Aquatic Resources, Spatial Analysis, and Systemic Modeling,* edited by Lewis Binford, pp. 385–96. New York: Academic Press, 1977.

Kessell, John L. "Diego Romero, the Plains Apaches, and the Inquisition." *The American West* 15 (May–June 1978), pp. 12–16.

———. *Kiva, Cross, and Crown: The Pecos Indians and New Mexico, 1540–1840.* Washington, D.C.: National Park Service, 1979.

———. "Esteban Clemente, Precursor of the Pueblo Revolt." *El Palacio* 86:4 (1980), pp. 16–17.

Lange, Charles H. "Relations of the Southwest with the Plains and Great Basin." In *Handbook of North American Indians, Volume 9: The Southwest,* edited by Alfonso Ortíz, pp. 201–205. Washington, D.C.: Smithsonian Institution.

Malvido, Elsa, and Carlos Viesca. "La epidemia de *cocoliztli* de 1576." *Historias* 1 (1985), pp. 27–34.

Moorhead, Max. *New Mexico's Royal Road.* Norman: University of Oklahoma Press, 1958.

Ortíz, Alfonso. "San Juan Pueblo." In *Handbook of North American Indians, Volume 9: The Southwest,* edited by Alfonso Ortíz, pp. 278–95. Washington, D.C.: Smithsonian Institution, 1979.

Reff, Daniel T. *Disease, Depopulation, and Culture Change in*

Northwestern New Spain, 1518–1764. Salt Lake City: University of Utah Press, 1991.

Ricard, Robert. *La "Conquête Sprituelle" du Mexique. Essai sur l'apostolat et les méthodes missionaires des ordres mendiants en Nouvelle-Espagne de 1523–24 à 1572.* Paris: Institut d'Ethnologie, 1933.

Roberts, Calvin, and Susan Roberts. *New Mexico.* Albuquerque: University of New Mexico Press, 1988.

Salmón, Roberto Mario. *Indian Revolts in Northern New Spain: A Synthesis of Resistance (1680–1786).* New York: University Press of America.

Sánchez, Jane C. "Spanish-Indian Relations during the Otermín Administration, 1677–1683." *New Mexico Historical Review* 58:2 (April 1983), pp. 133–51.

Sando, Joe. *The Pueblo Indians.* San Francisco: The Indian Historian Press, 1976.

———. "The Pueblo Revolt." In *Handbook of North American Indians, Volume 9: The Southwest,* edited by Alfonso Ortíz, pp. 194–97. Washington, D.C.: Smithsonian Institution, 1979.

———. *Pueblo Nations: Eight Centuries of Pueblo Indian History.* Santa Fe: Clear Light Publishers, 1992.

Scholes, France V. "The Supply Service of the New Mexican Missions in the Seventeenth Century." *New Mexico Historical Review* 5:1 (January 1930), pp. 93–115.

———. "Problems in the Early Ecclesiastical History of New Mexico." *New Mexico Historical Review* 7:1 (January 1932), pp. 32–74.

———. "Civil Government and Society in New Mexico in the Seventeenth Century." *New Mexico Historical Review* 10:2 (April 1935), pp. 71–111.

———. "The First Decade of the Inquisition in New Mexico." *New Mexico Historical Review* 10:3 (July 1935), pp. 195–241.

———. "Church and State in New Mexico, 1610–1650." *New Mexico Historical Review* 11:1 (January 1936), pp. 9–76;

11:2 (April 1936), pp. 145–78; 11:3 (July 1936), pp. 283–94; 11:4 (October 1936), pp. 297–349; and 12:1 (January 1937), pp. 78–106.

———. *Troublous Times in New Mexico, 1659–1670*. Albuquerque: Historical Society of New Mexico Publications in History, 1942.

———. "Juan Martinez de Montoya, Settler and Conquistador of New Mexico." *New Mexico Historical Review* 19:4 (October 1944), pp. 337–42.

Schroeder, Albert H. "Shifting for Survival in the Spanish Southwest." *New Mexico Historical Review* 43:4 (October 1968), pp. 291–310.

———. "Pueblos Abandoned in Historic Times." In *Handbook of North American Indians, Volume 9: The Southwest*, edited by Alfonso Ortiz, pp. 236–51. Washington, D.C.: Smithsonian Institution, 1979.

Simmons, Marc. "New Mexico's Smallpox Epidemic of 1780–1781." *New Mexico Historical Review* 41:1 (October 1966), pp. 319–26.

———. *New Mexico*. New York: W. W. Norton, 1977.

———. "History of Pueblo-Spanish Relations to 1821." In *Handbook of North American Indians, Volume 9: The Southwest*, edited by Alfonso Ortíz, pp. 178–223. Washington, D.C.: Smithsonian Institution, 1979.

Spicer, Edward. *Cycles of Conquest: The Impact of Spain, Mexico, and the United States on the Indians of the Southwest, 1533–1795*. Tucson: University of Arizona Press, 1962.

Stern, Steve J. *Peru's Indian Peoples and the Challenge of Spanish Conquest: Huamanga to 1640*. Madison: University of Wisconsin Press, 1982.

Thomas, David Hurst, ed. *Columbian Consequences, Volume I: Archaeological and Historical Perspectives on the Spanish Borderlands West*. Washington, D.C.: Smithsonian Institution Press, 1989.

Timmons, W. H. *El Paso: A Borderlands History*. El Paso: Texas

Western Press, 1990.

Tjarks, Alicia V. "Demographic, Ethnic, and Occupational Structure of New Mexico, 1790." *The Americas* 35 (1978–79), pp. 45–88.

Weber, David J. *The Spanish Frontier in North America.* New Haven: Yale University Press, 1992.

Wood, Peter H. "La Salle: Discovery of a Lost Explorer." *American Historical Review* 89:2 (April 1984), pp. 294–323.

Woodbury, Richard B., and Ezra B. W. Zubrow. "Agricultural Beginnings, 2000 B.C. to A.D. 500." In *Handbook of North American Indians, Volume 9: The Southwest,* edited by Alfonso Ortíz, pp. 43–60. Washington, D.C.: Smithsonian Institution, 1979.

Worcester, Donald E. "The Apaches in the History of the Southwest." *New Mexico Historical Review* 50:1 (January 1975), pp. 25–44.

Index

Boldface type indicates illustrations.